SPANISH FOR
HEALTH CARE
WORKBOOK

KAMMS Consulting, LLC
Ventnor, NJ 08406
www.spanishonthejob.com

Published by KAMMS Consulting, LLC
©2008 Stacey Kammerman-KAMMS Consulting, LLC
6715 Atlantic Avenue
Ventnor City, NJ 08406 U.S.A.
Manufactured in the U.S.A.
International Standard Book Number: 978-1-934842-39-3

contents

introduction

KAMMS PHILOSOPHY ABOUT LEARNING A NEW LANGUAGE FOR WORK

We believe that "it's all about communication". It's not necessary to become completely fluent, learn all the grammar rules and devote years studying a new language in order to immediately communicate and connect with people at work. All you need to do is learn the vocabulary and phrases that are essential for your job or profession!

Even though the company was founded by a certified Spanish teacher who has the knowledge to teach every detail about Spanish grammar, our philosophy for quickly learning Spanish for your job, contradicts this way of teaching a new language. We believe that learners who need essential Spanish for their job will be confident and successful if they are taught with communication as the *primary* focus of their language learning experience.

Many people have spent countless hours in a classroom setting or listening to language learning programs, trying to learn a new language with grammar rules, only to be disappointed and discouraged with the outcome; they can conjugate a verb, but they can't put a phrase or a sentence together in order to communicate. We want to change that!

We want every person to know that they can quickly and easily learn what they need to know in order to be successful and confident while communicating in a new language. Maybe more people would embark on a new language learning journey if they knew that it could be simple and that they could actually *use* what they have learned!

It really is quite simple! You learned to communicate in your first language without any stress or concern about the grammar and verb conjugations. You can do the same with a new language. That is the foundation of our job-specific language learning programs.

KAMMS' language programs provide an immediate, simple and effective solution to improve communication between English and Spanish speakers in the workplace.

BENEFITS OF LEARNING SPANISH FOR YOUR JOB OR PROFESSION

Over 500 million people in the world speak Spanish. In the US, Hispanics are the largest minority group; about 45 million. This large and growing population of Spanish-speakers in the U.S. and around the world has produced a workplace challenge. It is imperative for health care professionals to quickly learn survival Spanish for their job.

The benefits of learning Spanish for your job are numerous. We have compiled a list of immediate benefits health care professionals may experience. Once you start using your new language skills, you will probably notice even more than what's on this list!

> ➢ Improve Communication
> ➢ Improve Accuracy of Patient Diagnosis
> ➢ Advance Your Career
> ➢ Obtain a Better Job
> ➢ Increase Yours & Others' Safety
> ➢ Build Trust with Patients
> ➢ Gain Respect
> ➢ Be More Effective
> ➢ "Connect" with Spanish-Speakers & their family
> ➢ And Much More!

In addition to all of these benefits that you can achieve by learning Spanish for your job, you will be gaining an indispensable skill that will enrich your life!

LANGUAGE LEARNING TIPS

Take Your Time! When learning a new language it is best to practice for a short time each day. We suggest 30 minutes or 1 lesson a day. Continue with the same lesson until you have mastered it and then move on to the next.

Don't Be Shy! It is very important to use your new found language skills whenever possible. Unfortunately, some of us are stricken by "language ego". It is a term coined by Alexander Guiora (1981) to explain that people feel less confident when communicating in their second language. Don't worry; most people are thrilled that you are learning and using their native language and will do as much as possible to help you and make you feel more comfortable.

The other benefit of not "being shy" is that the person with whom you are speaking may also be "stricken" with language ego. When you speak a few words in their native language, they may feel more comfortable speaking to you in *their* second language.

Endings Make it Easy! The endings of many words in English correlate with the endings of many words in Spanish. If you learn these endings, you can quickly and easily add many words to your new vocabulary:

-ty = -dad:	university=universidad, activity=actividad
-tion = -ción:	attention=atención, vacation=vacación
-sion = -sión:	session=sesión, passion=pasión
-ive = -ivo:	active=activo, intensive=intensivo
-ly = -mente:	actively=activamente, effectively =efectivamente

"No" Makes it Easy! "No" is the same in Spanish and English. Additionally, (in Spanish) if you want to change something from a positive statement: "Yo corro."(I run.) to a negative statement: "Yo no corro." (I don't run.), all you have to do is put the word "no" in front of it.

Cognates Make it Easy! Here's great news for those of you learning Spanish; you can already "guess" 33% of the Spanish language. This is because 33% of the Spanish language is cognates. Cognates are words that look & sound similar in both Spanish and English: i.e. television=televisión, class=clase, professor=profesor

ABOUT KAMMS LANGUAGE PROGRAMS

You Can Quickly & Easily Learn the Necessary Language for a Specific Job or Profession

The average person takes up to five years to become fluent in a second language. Our programs give learners short and simple phrases that directly relate to the daily operations of their job, so they can immediately improve communication at work.

Repetition and Progression are Utilized throughout our Programs

Everyone knows that "repetition is the key to learning" and it is no different for learning a new language. The repetition and progression throughout our programs allow the learner to see/hear the same word many times while at the same time, we slowly introduce the new language one or two words at a time.

For example: Reporte...(Report...) Reporte los accidentes... (Report accidents...) Repórteme los accidentes. (Report accidents to me.)

Simplified Language Learning Process

Many of you may be familiar with the numerous (about 100) ways to conjugate a verb in Spanish. You will be pleased to know that we have simplified verb usage by mostly (whenever possible) using the formal (usted) form of the verb in Spanish and carefully choosing the English verb so as to make communication the main focus of our programs instead of grammar.

You may also be familiar with the masculine ("o" ending) and feminine ("a" ending) form of words and that there is a difference between "la" and "el". For example: **la** cas**a** blanc**a** and **el** sombrer**o** roj**o**. We have simplified this grammar rule for you by using the masculine form of all words throughout the program.

Phonetic Pronunciation Guide

A phonetic pronunciation guide is provided for every word and phrase presented in the KAMMS language programs. The words are divided by syllables with dashes and the stressed syllables are bold.

ABOUT KAMMS LANGUAGE PROGRAMS (CONT'D)

Each Lesson is Independent

Each lesson is independent of all other lessons. The lessons in each program do not build on the other lessons. This allows you to learn just the words and phrases that you need to know for a given situation.

Team of Language Experts

The qualifications of KAMMS' team of language acquisition experts range from degrees in the Spanish language, the English Language, Latin American Cultural Studies, Language Teaching Certifications and Certified Spanish Translators. In addition, the team has extensive experience teaching in schools businesses, various industries and government agencies. We are very fortunate to have many creative, innovative, knowledgeable and exceptional people on the KAMMS' team.

Grammar Only When Necessary

We teach grammar on the "need to know" basis. Throughout our programs you may see occasional explanations or activities that include grammar. We make it as brief as possible! There are certain circumstances that lend themselves to a grammar explanation and there are some learners that like knowing the explanation of the grammar. For this reason it is included in our programs when necessary.

Cognates Whenever Possible

Cognates are words that look and sound similar in Spanish and English (i.e. silencio=silence). In order to build on what you already know, we use cognates as much as possible throughout our language programs.

SPANISH PRONUNCIATION

Vowels (a, e, i, o, u)

Unlike English, the Spanish pronunciation of vowels remains consistent. There are no worries (like in English) about "long" vowels or "short" vowels. Vowels are typically pronounced clearly and distinctly. In other words, the vowel sounds are shorter and not "drawn out"; as in English. For example, the English "no" would be pronounced: nō-wa: whereas in Spanish it would be: nō. Here is a vowel pronunciation guide to follow:

a = ah: is similar to a in father

e = ā: is similar to a in day

i = ē: is similar to i in police

o = ō: is similar to o in note

u = oo: is similar to oo in school

Consonants

Most consonants (any letter other than a vowel is considered a consonant) sound the same in Spanish as they do in English. But there are additional letters in the Spanish alphabet and there are exceptions to the rules:

h is never pronounced, i.e. hola is pronounced ola

ñ is pronounced like the ny in canyon

rr is pronounced with a "roll" of the r

j is pronounced like the h in house

ll is pronounced like the y in yellow or j in Jamaica (depending on the speaker's country of origin)

Stress on Syllables

Words that end with a vowel, n, or s are stressed on the syllable before the last.
example: momento= mo-**men**-to

Some words have an accent mark which indicates the syllable that is stressed.
example: teléfono=te-**le**-fo-no

Sometimes words have accents simply to distinguish words.
example: él=he and el=the

Masculine and Feminine

In Spanish, the ending of some words will be an –**o** or an –**a** depending on whether you are speaking about a man or a woman.

   example: Maria es alt**a**. Carlos es alt**o**.

This also applies to "masculine" or "feminine" words in Spanish.

   example: cas**a** (it is feminine because it ends in "a") or sombrer**o** (it is masculine because it ends in "o").

Spanish also uses the articles-"la" and "una" before a feminine word and "el" and "un" before a masculine word.

   example: la cas**a** (the house)-una cas**a** (a house) el sombrer**o** (the hat)-un sombrer**o** (a hat)

The adjectives describing these words would also be feminine or masculine.

   example: la cas**a** blanc**a** (the white house)-el sombrer**o** roj**o** (the red hat)

Note: Not all nouns will end in o or a-and there are exceptions to the rules mentioned above.

   example: la corte (the court)-el arma (the weapon)

Plural Nouns

Words that end in a vowel become plural by adding "s".

   example: "la idea" becomes "las idea**s**"

Words that end in a consonant usually add "es".

   example: "la actividad" becomes "las actividad**es**"

Spanish Punctuation Marks

Additionally, you may notice the upside down exclamation point (¡) and the upside down question mark (¿). These are grammar marks that are not used in English but are used in Spanish.

CULTURE TIPS

Hispanic and Latino: Either term is acceptable to describe a person of Spanish descent; however most "Hispanics" prefer to be described by their country of origin, i.e. Mexican, Puerto Rican or Peruvian. There are over 20 Spanish-speaking countries in the world.

Spanish Surname System: Many Hispanics use two last names. The first last name is that of the father (apellido paterno) and the second is that of the mother (apellido materno).

example: Carlos Romero García

Señorita and Señora: Señorita is used when addressing a woman whose marital status is unknown, regardless of her age. Señora is used when addressing women who are married or women that are older than us.

Eye Contact: In the Hispanic culture, looking a person of authority in the eye may be considered disrespectful. It is considered a sign of respect to *not* make direct eye contact with a person of authority.

Commas & Decimals: In many Spanish speaking countries a period in numerals is used where English uses a comma and a comma is used to indicate the decimal where English uses a period.

example: $25,00=$25.00   5,9%=5.9%   10.000=10,000

Dates: Dates are written with the day first, then the month, and then the year. Also periods are used between the numbers.

example: 09/25/05 would be written: 25.09.05

September 25, 2005 would be written: el 25 de septiembre de 2005

Days of the Week and Months of the Year: The days of the week and the months of the year are not capitalized in Spanish.

LESSON 1

Commands (Mandatos)

come	venga (**behn**-gah)
come here	venga aquí (**behn**-gah ah-**kee**)
walk	camine (kah-**mee**-neh)
walk slowly	camine despacio (kah-**mee**-neh deh-**spah**-see-oh)
sit down	siéntese (see-**ehn**-teh-seh)
sit here	siéntese aquí (see-**ehn**-teh-seh ah-**kee**)
lie down	acuéstese (ah-koo-**eh**-steh-seh)
lie down here	acuéstese aquí (ah-koo-**eh**-steh-seh ah-**kee**)
lie on your back	acuéstese de espalda (ah-koo-**eh**-steh-seh deh eh-**spahl**-dah)
lie on your side	acuéstese de un lado (ah-koo-**eh**-steh-seh deh oon **lah**-doh)
stand up	levántese (leh-**bahn**-teh-seh)
don't stand up	no se levante (noh seh leh-**bahn**-teh)
wait	espere (eh-**spehr**-eh)
wait for me	espéreme (eh-**spehr**-eh-meh)

wait here	espére aquí (eh-**spehr**-eh ah-**kee**)
wait a moment	espére un momento (eh-**spehr**-eh oon moh-**mehn**-toh)
stop	pare (**pahr**-eh)
stop that	pare eso (**pahr**-eh **eh**-soh)
go	vaya (**bah**-yah)
go away	vaya afuera (**bah**-yah ah-foo-**wehr**-ah)
tell me	dígame (**dee**-gah-meh)
tell him/her	dígale (**dee**-gah-leh)
tell me what happened	dígame qué pasó (**dee**-gah-meh keh pah-**soh**)
say "ah"	díga "ah" (**dee**-gah ah)
give me	déme (**deh**-meh)
give me it	démelo (**deh**-meh-loh)
write	escriba (eh-**skree**-bah)
write it	escríbalo (eh-**skree**-bah-loh)
look	mire (**mee**-reh)

look here	mire aquí (*mee*-reh ah-*kee*)
look at me	míreme (*mee*-reh-meh)
look up	mire para arriba (*mee*-reh *pah*-rah ah-*rree*-bah)
look down	mire para abajo (*mee*-reh *pah*-rah ah-*bah*-hoh)
move	muévase (moo-*eh*-bah-seh)
don't move	no se mueva (noh seh moo-*eh*-bah)
move back	muévase para atrás (moo-*eh*-bah-seh *pah*-rah ah-*trahs*)
turn over	voltéese (bohl-*teh*-eh-seh)
bend	doble (*doh*-bleh)
bend your arm	doble el brazo (*doh*-bleh ehl *brah*-soh)
bend your leg	doble la pierna (*doh*-bleh lah pee-*ehr*-nah)
push	empuje (ehm-*poo*-heh)
don't push	no empuje (noh ehm-*poo*-heh)
be quiet	silencio (see-*lehn*-see-oh)
stay	quédese (*keh*-deh-seh)

©KAMMS Consulting, LLC   3

stay still	quédese quieto (**keh**-deh-seh kee-**eh**-toh)
stay in bed	quédese en la cama (**keh**-deh-seh ehn lah **kah**-mah)
close	cierre (see-**eh**-rreh)
close your eyes	cierre los ojos (see-**eh**-rreh lohs **oh**-hohs)
close your mouth	cierre la boca (see-**eh**-rreh lah **boh**-kah)
open	abra (**ah**-brah)
open your eyes	abra los ojos (**ah**-brah lohs **oh**-hohs)
open your mouth	abra la boca (**ah**-brah lah **boh**-kah)
stick out	saque (**sah**-keh)
stick out your tongue	saque la lengua (**sah**-keh lah **lehn**-goo-ah)
swallow	tráguese (**trah**-gueh-seh)
swallow it	trágueselo (**trah**-gueh-seh-loh)
breath	respire (reh-**spee**-reh)
breath like this	respire así (reh-**spee**-reh ah-**see**)
breathe normally	respire normalmente (reh-**spee**-reh nohr-mahl-**mehn**-teh)

breath deeply	respire profundo *(reh-**spee**-reh proh-**foon**-doh)*
breath slowly	respire despacio *(reh-**spee**-reh deh-**spah**-see-oh)*
cough	tosa *(**toh**-sah)*
follow	siga *(**see**-gah)*
follow me	sígame *(**see**-gah-meh)*
follow the instructions	siga las instrucciones *(**see**-gah lahs een-strook-see-**ohn**-ehs)*
again	otra vez *(**oh**-trah behs)*
be careful	cuidado *(koo-ee-**dah**-doh)*
put it	póngalo *(**pohn**-gah-loh)*
put it under	póngalo debajo *(**pohn**-gah-loh deh-**bah**-hoh)*
put it under your tongue	póngalo debajo de la lengua *(**pohn**-gah-loh deh-**bah**-hoh deh lah **lehn**-goo-ah)*
touch	toque *(**toh**-keh)*
don't touch	no toque *(noh **toh**-keh)*
point to	señale *(seh-**nyahl**-eh)*
point to it	señálelo *(seh-**nyahl**-eh-loh)*

show	enseñe *(ehn-**seh**-nyeh)*
show me	enséñeme *(ehn-**seh**-nyeh-meh)*
try	trate *(**trah**-teh)*
try it	trátelo *(**trah**-teh-loh)*
try to sleep	trate de dormir *(**trah**-teh deh door-**meer**)*
take	tome *(**toh**-meh)*
take the medicine	tome la medicina *(**toh**-meh lah meh-dee-**see**-nah)*
roll up	enrrólle *(ehn-**rroh**-yeh)*
roll up your sleeve	enrrólle la manga *(ehn-**rroh**-yeh lah **mahn**-gah)*
take off	quítese *(**kee**-teh-seh)*
take off your shirt	quítese su camisa *(**kee**-teh-seh soo kah-**mee**-sah)*
take off your pants	quítese sus pantalones *(**kee**-teh-seh soos pahn-teh-**loh**-nehs)*
take off your clothes	quítese su ropa *(**kee**-teh-seh soo **roh**-pah)*
wake up	despiértese *(dehs-pee-**ehr**-teh-seh)*
calm down	cálmese *(**kahl**-mah-seh)*

relax	relájase *(reh-**lah**-ha-seh)*
rest	descanse *(dehs-**kahn**-seh)*
don't worry	no se preocupe *(noh seh preh-oh-**koo**-peh)*
don't cry	no llore *(noh **yohr**-eh)*

LESSON 1

Ejercicios: Commands (Mandatos)

A. Tell the patient...

1. ... to close his / her eyes. → _____

2. ... to breathe deeply. → _____

3. ... to roll up his / her sleeve. → _____

4. ... to relax. → _____

5. ... to try to sleep. → _____

6. ... not to cry. → _____

7. ... to rest. → _____

8. ... not to worry. → _____

9. ... to sit down. → _____

10. ... to tell you what happened. → _____

B. Identify, from the list of words given, all of the terms that make reference to <u>body parts</u>.

mire	vaya afuera	quédese quieto
acuéstese de espalda	doble el brazo	respire
saque la lengua	abra los ojos	cálmese
quítese sus pantalones	póngalo debajo de la lengua	doble la pierna
silencio	cierre los ojos	cierre la boca

1. _____

2. _____

3. _____

4. _____

5. _____

6. _____

7. _____

8. _____

C. Translate the suggested sentences by making combinations with expressions from columns A and B.

A:	B:
_ Venga	_ aquí.
_ Camine	_ despacio.
_ Siéntese	_ afuera.
_ Acuéstese	_ para arriba.
_ Espere	_ para abajo.
_ Vaya	_ para atrás.
_ Mire	_ así.
_ Respire	_ normalmente.
_ Póngalo	_ profundo.
_ Voltéese	_ debajo.

1. Put it under. → _____

2. Breathe slowly. → _____

3. Sit here. → _____

4. Come here. → _____

5. Walk normally. → _____

6. Lie down here. → _____

7. Wait outside. → _____

8. Look up. → _____

9. Breathe deeply. → _____

10. Turn over slowly. → _____

11. Go outside / away. → _____

12. Look down. → _____

13. Come slowly. → _____

14. Walk like this. → _____

15. Sit outside. → _____

16. Look back. → _____

D. Choose the most appropriate option to finish the sentences.

1. Espere ...
a. la lengua   b. los pantalones   c. un momento

2. Quédese ...
a. la boca   b. en la cama   c. la medicina

3. Siga ...
a. las instrucciones   b. la manga   c. un momento

4. Tome ...
a. otra vez   b. la medicina   c. tosa

5. Quítese ...
a. preocupe   b. su camisa   c. cuidado

E. Now, translate the sentences you just built. The first letter of the verb is already written.

1. W _____ .

2. S _____ .

3. F _____ .

4. T _____ .

5. T _____ .

F. Fill in the missing vowels to make these basic commands.

1. L _ V _ N T _ S _ → stand up
2. P _ R _ → stop
3. D _ G _ M _ → tell me
4. D _ M _ → give me
5. _ S C R _ B _ → write
6. M _ _ V _ S _ → move
7. D _ B L _ → bend
8. _ M P _ J _ → push
9. S _ L _ N C _ _ → be quiet
10. Q _ _ D _ S _ → stay

11. C _ _ R R _ → close
12. _ B R _ → open
13. S _ Q _ _ → stick out
14. T R _ G _ _ S _ → swallow
15. T _ S _ → cough
16. T _ Q _ _ → touch
17. S _ Ñ _ L _ → point to
18. _ N S _ Ñ _ → show
19. T R _ T _ → try
20. D _ S P _ _ R T _ S _ → wake up

G. Match the two columns.

1. Descanse.	a. Come.
2. No llore.	b. Stick out your tongue.
3. Dígale.	c. Breathe slowly.
4. Silencio.	d. Don't cry.
5. Tome la medicina.	e. Write it.
6. Camine despacio.	f. Rest.
7. Respire normalmente.	g. Lie on your back.
8. Trate de dormir.	h. Stay in bed.
9. Escríbalo.	i. Take the medicine.
10. Cierre los ojos.	j. Don't worry.
11. Cálmese.	k. Walk slowly.
12. Espere un momento.	l. Look up.
13. Saque la lengua.	m. Try to sleep.
14. Siga las instrucciones.	n. Calm down.
15. Acuéstese de espalda.	o. Tell him/her.
16. Quédese en la cama.	p. Bend your leg.
17. Respire despacio.	q. Follow the instructions.
18. Vaya afuera.	r. Wait a moment.
19. Mire para arriba.	s. Close your eyes.
20. Quítese sus pantalones.	t. Put it under your tongue.
21. Dígame qué pasó.	u. Go away.
22. Doble la pierna.	v. Be quiet.
23. Póngalo debajo de la lengua.	w. Take off your pants.
24. Venga.	x. Tell me what happened.
25. No se preocupe.	y. Breathe normally.

H. Review the pronunciation section of this lesson's vocabulary. Say the words in Spanish, transcribe them into Spanish & write their meaning.

| example: *see-**ehn**-teh-seh* → siéntese→ sit down |

1. *bohl-**teh**-eh-seh* →   →

2. *noh **toh**-keh* →   →

3. *eh-**skree**-bah* →   →

4. *ah-brah* →   →

5. *koo-ee-**dah**-doh* →   →

6. **deh**-meh →   →

7. **trah**-gueh-seh →   →

8. ehn-**seh**-nyeh →   →

9. noh seh leh-**bahn**-teh →   →

10. moo-**eh**-bah-seh →   →

11. ehn-**rroh**-yeh lah **mahn**-gah →   →

12. eh-**spehr**-eh-meh →   →

13. reh-**spee**-reh ah-**see** →   →

14. seh-**nyahl**-eh →   →

15. **pahr**-eh eh-**soh** →   →

16. **keh**-deh-seh kee-**eh**-toh →   →

17. dehs-pee-**ehr**-teh-seh →   →

18. see-**ehn**-teh-seh ah-**kee** →   →

19. noh ehm-**poo**-heh →   →

20. **toh**-sah →   →

21. **see**-gah →   →

22. **dee**-gah ah →   →

23. **doh**-bleh ehl **brah**-soh →   →

24. reh-**lah**-ha-seh →   →

©KAMMS Consulting, LLC

LESSON 2

Meeting the Patient (La Reunión con el Paciente)

My name is...	Me llamo... *(meh yah-moh)*
I am...	Soy... *(soo-ee)*
I am the doctor.	Soy el (la) doctor(a). *(soo-ee ehl (lah) dohk-tohr(ah))*
I am the nurse.	Soy el (la) enfermero(a). *(soo-ee ehl (lah) ehn-fehr-mehr-oh(ah))*
I am the assistant.	Soy el (la) ayudante. *(soo-ee ehl (lah) ah-yoo-dahn-teh)*
I am the paramedic.	Soy el (la) paramédico. *(soo-ee ehl (lah) pah-rah-meh-dee-koh)*
What is your name?	¿Cómo se llama? *(koh-moh seh yah-mah)*
Why?	¿Por qué? *(pohr-keh)*
Why are you here?	¿Por qué está aquí? *(pohr-keh eh-stah ah-kee)*
Help!	¡Ayuda! *(ah-yoo-da)*
Do you need help?	¿Necesita ayuda? *(neh-seh-see-tah ah-yoo-da)*
Who needs help?	¿Quién necesita ayuda? *(kee-ehn neh-seh-see-tah ah-yoo-da)*
I can help.	Puedo ayudar. *(poo-eh-doh ah-yoo-dahr)*
We are going to help.	Vamos a ayudar. *(bah-mohs ah ah-yoo-dahr)*

| Are you...? | ¿Está...? |
| | *(eh-__stah__)* |

| Are you OK? | ¿Está bien? |
| | *(eh-__stah bee__-ehn)* |

| Are you sick? | ¿Está enfermo(a)? |
| | *(eh-__stah__ ehn-__fehr__-moh(ah))* |

| Are you hurt? | ¿Está lastimado(a)? |
| | *(eh-__stah__ lah-stee-__mah__-doh(ah))* |

| Who is hurt? | ¿Quién está lastimado(a)? |
| | *(kee-__ehn__ eh-__stah__ lah-stee-__mah__-doh(ah))* |

| Do you speak English? | ¿Habla inglés? |
| | *(__ah__-blah een-__glehs__)* |

| I speak a little Spanish. | Hablo un poco de español. |
| | *(__ah__-bloh oon __poh__-koh deh ehs-pah-__nyol__)* |

| I don't understand. | No entiendo. |
| | *(noh ehn-tee-__ehn__-doh)* |

| Do you understand? | ¿Entiende? |
| | *(ehn-tee-__ehn__-deh)* |

| Speak slowly. | Hable despacio. |
| | *(__ah__-bleh dehs-__pah__-see-oh)* |

| It is necessary. | Es necesario. |
| | *(ehs neh-seh-__sah__-ree-oh)* |

| It is not important. | No es importante. |
| | *(noh ehs eem-pohr-__tahn__-teh)* |

| You are doing fine. | Está bien. |
| | *(eh-__stah bee__-ehn)* |

| Everything is fine. | Todo está bien. |
| | *(__toh__-doh eh-__stah bee__-ehn)* |

| I have questions. | Tengo preguntas. |
| | *(__tehn__-goh preh-__goon__-tahs)* |

| I need to examine you. | Necesito examinarlo (a). |
| | *(neh-seh-__see__-toh eks-ah-mee-__nahr__-loh(lah))* |

Lesson 2

Ejercicios: Meeting the Patient (La Reunión con el Paciente)

A. Fill in the blank with the correct word to complete the sentences.

1. Everything is fine. → *Todo está* _____.
          a.) *enfermo*   b.) *bien*   c.) *fino*   d.) *aquí*

2. Speak slowly. → _____ *despacio.*
          a.) *Enfermo*   b.) *Necesita*   c) *Hable*   d.) *Soy*

3. I need to examine you. → _____ *examinarlo(a).*
          a.) *Entiendo*   b.) *Hablo*   c.) *Tengo*   d.) *Necesito*

4. We are going to help. → *Vamos a* _____.
          a.) *está*   b.) *cómo*   c.) *ayudar*   d.) *hablar*

5. I have questions. → *Tengo* _____.
          a.) *preguntas*   b.) *llama*   c.) *importante*   d.) *lastimada*

6. Who needs help? → ¿_____ *necesita ayuda?*
          a.) *Soy*   b.) *Entiende*   c.) *Por qué*   d.) *Quién*

7. I speak a little Spanish. → _____ *un poco de Español.*
          a.) *Hable*   b.) *Hablo*   c.) *Habla*   d.) *Necesito*

8. I don't understand. → *No* _____.
          a.) *entiende*   b.) *entiendo*   c.) *necesito*   d.) *necesita*

9. I am the assistant. → _____ *el ayudante.*
          a.) *Está*   b.) *Por qué*   c) *Soy*   d.) *Quién*

10. Are you sick? → ¿*Está* _____?
          a.) *lastimado*   b.) *bien*   c.) *despacio*   d.) *enfermo*

11. Why are you here? → ¿_____ *está aquí?*
          a.) *Quién*   b.) *Por qué*   c.) *Todo*   d.) *Qué*

12. I can help. → _____ *ayudar.*
          a.) *Necesito*   b.) *Hablo*   c.) *Puedo*   d.) *Vamos*

13. It is necessary. → *Es* _____.
          a.) *necesario*   b.) *necesito*   c.) *necesita*   d.) *importante*

14. Are you hurt? → ¿*Está* _____?
          a.) *lastimado*   b.) *bien*   c.) *despacio*   d.) *enfermo*

15. What is your name? → ¿_____ se llama?
   a.) *Quién*   b.) *Por qué*   c.) *Está*   d.) *Cómo*

B. Unscramble the words to make meaningful sentences.

1. necesita / ¿Quién / ayuda? →
_____

2. doctor / Soy / el (la) →
_____

3. importante / es / No →
_____

4. examinarlo(a) / Necesito →
_____

5. bien / está / Todo →
_____

6. está / ¿Por / qué / aquí? →
_____

7. lastimado(a)? / está / ¿Quién →
_____

8. de / español / poco / un / Hablo →
_____

9. llama? / ¿Cómo / se →
_____

10. el(la) / Soy / ayudante →
_____

C. Now, translate the sentences you just built.

1._____
2._____
3._____
4._____
5._____

6._____

7._____

8._____

9._____

10._____

D. *I can help!* Exchange the first words with a car accident victim.

1. My name is <u>(your name)</u> →

....

2. I speak a little Spanish.   →

....

3. I am the paramedic.   →

....

4. We are going to help.   →

....

5. Are you hurt?   →

....

6. I need to examine you.   →

....

7. It is necessary.   →

....

8. I have questions.   →

....

9. Speak slowly.   →

....

10. I don't understand.   →

....

11. You are doing fine.   →

....

E. Choose (from the box) the English version of the words provided.

I am the nurse.	I am the assistant.
I don't understand.	It is not important.
Everything is fine.	I have questions.
I can help.	Why?
Help	Speak slowly.

1. Ayuda. →

_____

2. Puedo ayudar. →

_____

3. Soy el (la) enfermero. →

_____

4. Soy el (la) ayudante. →

_____

5. No entiendo. →

_____

6. No es importante. →

_____

7. ¿Por qué? →

_____

8. Hable despacio. →

_____

9. Tengo preguntas. →

_____

10. Todo está bien. →

_____

F. Ask the right questions! Choose the most appropriate question for every situation.

1. You want to know if the patient is sick.
a. ¿Entiende?   b. ¿Está enfermo?   c. ¿Cómo se llama?

2. Ask the patient if he / she speaks English.
a. ¿Está bien?   b. ¿Por qué está aquí?   c. ¿Habla inglés?

3. Ask the patient if he / she understands what you have said.
a. ¿Entiende?   b. ¿Está enfermo?   c. ¿Por qué?

4. Ask the patient if he / she needs help.
a. ¿Necesita ayuda?   b. ¿Quién necesita ayuda?   c. ¿Cómo se llama?

5. Ask the patient if he / she is OK.
a. ¿Está enfermo?   b. ¿Está bien?   c. ¿Está lastimado(a)?

6. Ask the patient if he is hurt.
a. ¿Está lastimado?   b. ¿Es necesario?   c. ¿Está bien?

7. Ask the patient why she is here.
a. ¿Necesita ayuda?   b. ¿Quién necesita ayuda?   c. ¿Por qué está aqui?

8. Ask who needs help.
a. ¿Está lastimado?   b. ¿Por qué está aquí?   c. ¿Quién necesita ayuda?

9. Ask: "Who is hurt?"
a. ¿Quién está lastimado?   b. ¿Está lastimado?   c. ¿Está enfermo?

10. Ask the patient his/her name.
a. ¿Habla inglés?   b. ¿Cómo se llama?   c. ¿Entiende?

G. Study the pronunciation section in your vocabulary. Say the words in Spanish, transcribe them into Spanish and write what they mean in English.

1. *eh-**stah bee**-ehn* →

_____ /

_____

2. *soo-**ee** ehl (lah) dohk-**tohr**(ah)* →

_____ /

_____

3. *noh ehs eem-pohr-**tahn**-teh* →

_____ /

_____

4. ***koh**-moh seh **yah**-mah* →

_____ /

_____

5. *meh **yah**-moh* →

_____ /

_____

6. ***tehn**-goh preh-**goon**-tahs* →

_____ /

_____

7. *neh-seh-**see**-tah ah-yoo-**da*** →

_____ /

_____

8. ***ah**-bloh oon **poh**-koh deh ehs-pah-**nyol*** →

_____ /

_____

9. ***bah**-mohs ah ah-yoo-**dahr*** →

_____ /

_____

10. *neh-seh-**see**-toh eks-ah-mee-**nahr**-loh(lah)* →

_____ /

_____

11. *noh ehn-tee-**ehn**-doh* →

_____ /

_____

12. *eh-**stah** lah-stee-**mah**-doh(ah)* →

_____ /

_____

13. *soo-**ee** ehl (lah) ah-yoo-**dahn**-teh* →

_____ /

_____

©KAMMS Consulting, LLC

14. **ah**-bleh dehs-**pah**-see-oh →
_____ /
_____

15. ehs neh-seh-**sah**-ree-oh →
_____ /
_____

16. **ah**-blah een-**glehs** →
_____ /
_____

17. pohr-**keh** eh-**stah** ah-**kee** →
_____ /
_____

18. **toh**-doh eh-**stah** bee-ehn →
_____ /
_____

19. kee-**ehn** neh-seh-**see**-tah ah-yoo-**da** →
_____ /
_____

20. soo-**ee** ehl (lah) ehn-fehr-**mehr**-oh(ah) →
_____ /
_____

LESSON 3

What the Patient Would Say (*Qué Diría el Paciente*)

Help!	¡Ayuda! *(ah-**yoo**-dah)*
Help me!	¡Ayúdame! *(ah-**yoo**-da-meh)*
Help him/her!	¡Ayúdale! *(ah-**yoo**-da-leh)*
pain	dolor *(doh-**lohr**)*
I have pain.	Tengo dolor. *(**tehn**-goh doh-**lohr**)*
I have severe pain.	Tengo dolor fuerte. *(**tehn**-goh doh-**lohr** foo-**ehr**-teh)*
I have chest pain.	Tengo dolor en el pecho. *(**tehn**-goh doh-**lohr** ehn ehl **peh**-choh)*
It hurts.	Me duele. *(meh doo-**eh**-leh)*
It hurts a lot.	Me duele mucho. *(meh doo-**eh**-leh **moo**-choh)*
It hurts here.	Me duele aquí. *(meh doo-**eh**-leh ah-**kee**)*
It hurts when I breathe.	Me duele al respirar. *(meh doo-**eh**-leh ahl reh-spee-**rahr**)*
I'm hurt.	Estoy lastimado(a). *(eh-**stoo**-ee lah-stee-**mah**-doh(dah))*
He/she is hurt.	Está lastimado(a). *(eh-**stah** lah-stee-**mah**-doh(dah))*
It burns.	Me quema. *(meh **keh**-mah)*

It burns here.	Me quema aquí. *(meh **keh**-mah ah-**kee**)*
It itches.	Me pica. *(meh **pee**-kah)*
It itches here.	Me pica aquí. *(meh **pee**-kah ah-**kee**)*
blood	sangre *(**sahn**-greh)*
I'm bleeding.	Estoy sangrando. *(eh-**stoo**-ee sahn-**grahn**-doh)*
He/she is bleeding.	Está sangrando. *(eh-**stah** sahn-**grahn**-doh)*
I'm sick.	Estoy enfermo(a). *(eh-**stoo**-ee ehn-**fehr**-moh(ah))*
He/she is sick.	Está enfermo(a). *(eh-**stah** ehn-**fehr**-moh(ah))*
I fell.	Me caí. *(meh kah-**ee**)*
He/she fell.	Se cayó. *(seh kah-**yoh**)*
I can't.	No puedo. *(noh poo-**eh**-doh)*
I can't breathe.	No puedo respirar. *(noh poo-**eh**-doh reh-spee-**rahr**)*
I can't sleep.	No puedo dormir. *(noh poo-**eh**-doh dohr-**meer**)*
I can't eat.	No puedo comer. *(noh poo-**eh**-doh koh-**mehr**)*

I can't move.	No puedo moverme. *(noh poo-**eh**-doh moh-**behr**-meh)*
I don't know.	No sé. *(noh seh)*
I'm afraid.	Tengo miedo. *(**tehn**-goh mee-**eh**-doh)*
I have an allergy.	Tengo alergia. *(**tehn**-goh ah-**lehr**-he-ah)*
I need...	Necesito... *(neh-seh-**see**-toh)*
I want...	Quiero... *(kee-**eh**-roh)*
Am I going to die?	¿Me voy a morir? *(meh **boh**-ee ah mohr-**eer**)*
Is he/she going to die?	¿Se va a morir? *(seh bah ah mohr-**eer**)*
What are you doing?	¿Qué hace? *(keh **ah**-seh)*
Do you know?	¿Usted sabe? *(oo-**stehd sah**-beh)*

Lesson 3

Ejercicios: What the Patient Would Say (Qué Diría el Paciente)

A. What are they telling you?

1. Me duele al respirar.

a. He / she is sick.   b. I have severe pain.   c. It hurts when I breathe.

2. Estoy sangrando.

a. It burns here.   b. I have an allergy.   c. I am bleeding.

3. No puedo moverme.

a. I am afraid.   b. I can't move.   c. Do you know?

4. ¿Se va a morir?

a. What are you doing?   b. Do you know?   c. Is he / she going to die?

5. ¡Ayúdame!

a. I fell!   b. Help me!   c. Help him / her!

6. Me quema aquí.

a. It hurts a lot.   b. It burns here.   c. It itches here.

7. Tengo dolor en el pecho.

a. I have pain.   b. I have severe pain.   c. I have chest pain.

8. Se cayó.

a. It hurts.   b. He / she fell.   c. I can't.

9. Tengo alergia.

a. I'm afraid.   b. I don't know.   c. I have an allergy.

10. No puedo comer.

a. I can't sleep.   b. I can't eat.   c. I can't breathe.

B. You are the patient now. Say in Spanish...

1. Help! →

_____

2. I have severe pain. →

_____

3. It hurts a lot here. →

_____

4. I fell. →

_____

5. I can't breathe. →

_____

6. I need ... →

_____

7. I want... →

_____

8. Do you know?

_____

9. What are you doing? →

_____

10. I don't know. →

_____

C. Predict the statements you will get from a patient in these situations.

1. This person is telling you that something hurts.

_____

2. This person is scratching her neck and points at it.

_____

3. This person is pointing at his sickly-looking sister.

_____

4. This person looks like he has not slept in days.

_____

5. This person looks anxiety-ridden and is worried about dying.

_____

6. You told this person to bend his leg but he does not seem to be able to do it.

_____

7. This person is pointing at someone who is bleeding.

_____

8. After a fire, this person points at his burnt leg and says this.

_____

9. After an accident, this person points at his injured co-worker and says this.

_____

10. This person is asking you to help the victim of a car crash.

_____

D. Choose (from the box) the correct translation for these expressions and write it in the space provided.

Do you know?	I can't breathe.	Am I going to die?	It itches here.
I'm afraid.	It hurts when I breathe.	I have an allergy.	I can't sleep.
Help!	I have chest pain.	He/she fell.	What are you doing?
I have pain.	I have severe pain	It burns here.	I am sick.
I can't move.	I am bleeding.	I am hurt.	I can't eat.

1. Se cayó. → _____

2. Tengo alergia. → _____

3. No puedo dormir. → _____

4. Me duele al respirar. → _____

5. Tengo dolor en el pecho. → _____

6. No puedo moverme. → _____

7. ¿Usted sabe? → _____

8. Estoy sangrando. → _____

9. ¡Ayuda! → _____

10. Me quema aquí. → _____

11. Estoy enfermo. → _____

12. ¿Me voy a morir? → _____

13. Tengo miedo. → _____

14. Tengo dolor. → _____

15. No puedo respirar. → _____

16. ¿Qué hace? → _____

17. Me pica aquí. → _____

18. No puedo comer. → _____

19. Tengo dolor fuerte. → _____

20. Estoy lastimado. → _____

E. Study the pronunciation section in your vocabulary. Say the word in Spanish, transcribe it into Spanish and write the meaning.

1. *ah-**yoo**-da-meh* →
_____ /
_____

2. ***sahn**-greh* →
_____ /
_____

3. *noh seh* →
_____ /
_____

4. *noh poo-**eh**-doh* →
_____ /
_____

5. *meh doo-**eh**-leh **moo**-choh* →
_____ /
_____

6. *eh-**stah** ehn-**fehr**-moh(ah)* →
_____ /
_____

7. *meh **keh**-mah* →
_____ /
_____

8. *ah-**yoo**-da-leh* →
_____ /
_____

9. *neh-seh-**see**-toh* →

_____ /

_____

10. *seh bah ah mohr-**eer*** →

_____ /

_____

11. *meh kah-**ee*** →

_____ /

_____

12. *meh doo-**eh**-leh* →

_____ /

_____

13. *meh **pee**-kah* →

_____ /

_____

14. *eh-**stah** sahn-**grahn**-doh* →

_____ /

_____

15. *meh doo-**eh**-leh ah-**kee*** →

_____ /

_____

16. *eh-**stah** lah-stee-**mah**-doh(dah)* →

_____ /

_____

17. *kee-**eh**-roh* →

_____ /

_____

18. *doh-**lohr*** →

_____ /

_____

19. *seh kah-**yoh*** →

_____ /

_____

20. *keh **ah**-seh* →

_____ /

_____

LESSON 4

Questions for the Patient (Preguntas para el Paciente)

Does it hurt?	¿Le duele? *(leh doo-**eh**-leh)*
Where does it hurt?	¿Dónde le duele? *(**dohn**-deh leh doo-**eh**-leh)*
Show me...	Enséñeme... *(ehn-**seh**-nyah-meh)*
Show me where it hurts.	Enséñeme dónde le duele. *(ehn-**seh**-nyah-meh **dohn**-deh leh doo-**eh**-leh)*
a lot or a little	mucho o poco *(**moo**-choh oh **poh**-koh)*
Does it hurt a lot or a little?	¿Le duele mucho o poco? *(leh doo-**eh**-leh **moo**-choh oh **poh**-koh)*
Does it hurt when I press?	¿Le duele cuando presiono? *(leh doo-**eh**-leh koo-**ahn**-doh preh-see-**oh**-noh)*
Did someone hurt you?	¿Lo/la lastimó alguien? *(loh(lah) lah-stee-**moh** ahl-**gee**-ehn)*
Where is he/she?	¿Dónde está? *(**dohn**-deh eh-**stah**)*
Where is the weapon?	¿Dónde está el arma? *(**dohn**-deh eh-**stah** ehl **ahr**-mah)*
When?	¿Cuándo? *(koo-**ahn**-doh)*
When did it happen?	¿Cuándo ocurrió? *(koo-**ahn**-doh oh-kohr-ee-**oh**)*
When did it start?	¿Cuándo empezó? *(koo-**ahn**-doh ehm-peh-**soh**)*

How much?	¿Cuánto? *(koo-**ahn**-toh)*
How much time?	¿Cuánto tiempo? *(koo-**ahn**-toh tee-**ehm**-poh)*
How long ago?	¿Por cuánto tiempo? *(pohr koo-**ahn**-toh tee-**ehm**-poh)*
How much do you weigh?	¿Cuánto pesa ? *(koo-**ahn**-toh **peh**-sah)*
How often?	¿Con qué frequencia? *(kohn keh freh-koo-**ehn**-see-ah)*
In what part?	¿En qué parte? *(ehn keh **pahr**-teh)*
What were you doing?	¿Qué estaba haciendo? *(**keh** eh-**stah**-bah ah-see-**ehn**-doh)*
Were you unconscious?	¿Estaba inconsiente? *(eh-**stah**-bah een-kohn-see-**ehn**-teh)*
How many?	¿Cuántos? *(koo-**ahn**-tohs)*
How many hours?	¿Cuántas horas? *(koo-**ahn**-tahs **ohr**-ahs)*
How many days?	¿Cuántos días? *(koo-**ahn**-tohs **dee**-ahs)*
How many weeks?	¿Cuántas semanas? *(koo-**ahn**-tahs seh-**mahn**-ahs)*
How many pills?	¿Cuántas pastillas? *(koo-**ahn**-tahs pah-**stee**-yahs)*
What?	¿Qué? *(keh)*
What did you eat?	¿Qué comió? *(keh koh-mee-**oh**)*

What did you drink/take?	¿Qué tomó? *(keh toh-**moh**)*
What is happening to you?	¿Qué le pasa? *(keh leh **pah**-sah)*
your symptoms	sus síntomas *(soos **seen**-toh-mahs)*
What are your symptoms?	¿Cuáles son sus síntomas? *(koo-**ahl**-ehs sohn soos **seen**-toh-mahs)*
Do you want...?	¿Quiere...? *(kee-**eh**-reh)*
Do you want something?	¿Quiere algo? *(kee-**eh**-reh **ahl**-goh)*
Do you want something to eat?	¿Quiere algo de comer? *(kee-**eh**-reh **ahl**-goh deh koh-**mehr**)*
Do you want something to drink?	¿Quiere algo de tomar? *(kee-**eh**-reh **ahl**-goh deh toh-**mahr**)*
Do you want something for pain?	¿Quiere algo para el dolor? *(kee-**eh**-reh **ahl**-goh **pah**-rah ehl doh-**lohr**)*
Do you want to go to the hospital?	¿Quiere ir al hospital? *(kee-**eh**-reh eer ahl oh-spee-**tahl**)*
Do you need...?	¿Necesita...? *(neh-seh-**see**-tah)*
Do you need an appointment?	¿Necesita una cita? *(neh-seh-**see**-tah **oon**-ah **see**-tah)*
Do you need to go to the hospital?	¿Necesita ir al hospital? *(neh-seh-**see**-tah eer ahl oh-speh-**tahl**)*

Do you need to go to the bathroom?

¿Necesita ir al baño?
*(neh-seh-**see**-tah eer ahl **bah**-nyoh)*

How?

¿Cómo?
*(**koh**-moh)*

How do you feel?

¿Cómo se siente?
*(**koh**-moh seh see-**ehn**-teh)*

How did it happen?

¿Cómo ocurrió?
*(**koh**-moh oh-koo-rree-**oh**)*

accident

accidente
*(ahks-see-**dehn**-teh)*

Was it an accident?

¿Fue un accidente?
*(**foo**-eh oon ahks-see-**dehn**-teh)*

Did you fall?

¿Se cayó?
*(seh kah-**yoh**)*

Do you have...?

¿Tiene...?
*(tee-**eh**-neh)*

Do you have a problem?

¿Tiene un problema?
*(tee-**eh**-neh oon proh-**bleh**-mah)*

Do you have chills?

¿Tiene escalofrios?
*(tee-**eh**-neh eh-skah-loh-**free**-ohs)*

Do you have nausea?

¿Tiene náusea?
*(tee-**eh**-neh **nah**-oo-see-ah)*

Do you have allergies?

¿Tiene alergias?
*(tee-**eh**-neh ah-**lehr**-he-ahs)*

Do you have an allergy to penicillian?

¿Tiene alergia a la penicilina?
*(tee-**eh**-neh ah-**lehr**-he-ah ah lah pehn-ee-see-**leen**-ah)*

Do you have allergies to any medicines?

¿Tiene alergias a alguna medicinas?
*(tee-**eh**-neh ah-**lehr**-he-ahs ah ahl-**goon**-ah meh-dee-**seen**-ahs)*

Do you have numbness?	¿Tiene adormecimiento? *(tee-**eh**-neh ah-dohr-meh-see-mee-**ehn**-toh)*
Do you have contractions?	¿Tiene contracciones? *(tee-**eh**-neh kohn-trahk-see-**oh**-nehs)*
Do you have pain?	¿Tiene dolor? *(tee-**eh**-neh doh-**lohr**)*
Do you have a headache?	¿Tiene dolor de cabeza? *(tee-**eh**-neh doh-**lohr** deh kah-**beh**-sah)*
Do you have chest pain?	¿Tiene dolor en el pecho? *(tee-**eh**-neh doh-**lohr** ehn ehl **peh**-choh)*
Do you have a stomachache?	¿Tiene dolor de estómago? *(tee-**eh**-neh doh-**lohr** deh eh-**stoh**-mah-goh)*
Do you have back pain?	¿Tiene dolor de la espalda? *(tee-**eh**-neh doh-**lohr** deh lah eh-**spahl**-dah)*
Do you have testicular pain?	¿Tiene dolor en los testículos? *(tee-**eh**-neh doh-**lohr** ehn lohs teh-**stee**-koo-lohs)*
Do you have difficulty?	¿Tiene dificultad? *(tee-**eh**-neh dee-fee-kool-**tahd**)*
Do you have difficulty swallowing?	¿Tiene dificultad para tragar? *(tee-**eh**-neh dee-fee-kool-**tahd pah**-rah trah-**gahr**)*
Do you have difficulty breathing?	¿Tiene dificultad para respirar? *(tee-**eh**-neh dee-fee-kool-**tahd pah**-rah reh-spee-**rahr**)*
Do you have difficulty urinating?	¿Tiene dificultad para orinar? *(tee-**eh**-neh dee-fee-kool-**tahd pah**-rah ohr-ee-**nahr**)*
Do you have difficulty defecating?	¿Tiene dificultad para defecar? *(tee-**eh**-neh dee-fee-kool-**tahd pah**-rah deh-feh-**kahr**)*

Are you hungry?	¿Tiene hambre? *(tee-**eh**-neh **ahm**-breh)*
Are you thirsty?	¿Tiene sed? *(tee-**eh**-neh sehd)*
Are you cold?	¿Tiene frío? *(tee-**eh**-neh **free**-oh)*
Are you hot?	¿Tiene calor? *(tee-**eh**-neh kah-**lohr**)*
Do you take...	¿Toma...? *(**toh**-mah)*
Do you take medicines?	¿Toma medicinas? *(**toh**-mah meh-dee-**see**-nahs)*
Do you take pills?	¿Toma pastillas? *(**toh**-mah pah-**stee**-yahs)*
Do you take illegal drugs?	¿Toma drogas ilegales? *(**toh**-mah **droh**-gahs ee-lee-**gah**-lehs)*
Do you drink alcohol?	¿Toma alcohol? *(**toh**-mah ahl-koh-**ohl**)*
Do you drink coffee?	¿Toma café? *(**toh**-mah kah-**feh**)*
Do you take vitamins?	¿Toma vitaminas? *(**toh**-mah bee-tah-**mee**-nahs)*
Did you take...	¿Tomó...? *(toh-**moh**)*
Did you take something?	¿Tomó algo? *(toh-**moh** **ahl**-goh)*
Did you take medicine?	¿Tomó medicina? *(toh-**moh** meh-dee-**see**-nah)*
Did you take the wrong medicine?	¿Tomó la medicina incorrecta? *(toh-**moh** lah meh-dee-**see**-nah een-koh-**rrehk**-tah)*

Did you take too much medicine?	¿Tomó demasiada medicina? *(toh-**moh** deh-mah-see-**ah**-dah meh-dee-**see**-nah)*
Are you cold?	¿Tiene frío? *tee-**eh**-neh **free**-oh)*
Are you hot?	¿Tiene calor? *(tee-**eh**-neh kah-**lohr**)*
Do you take...	¿Toma...? *(**toh**-mah)*
Do you take medicines?	¿Toma medicinas? *(**toh**-mah meh-dee-**see**-nahs)*
Do you take pills?	¿Toma pastillas? *(**toh**-mah pah-**stee**-yahs)*
Do you take illegal drugs?	¿Toma drogas ilegales? *(**toh**-mah **droh**-gahs ee-lee-**gah**-lehs)*
Do you drink alcohol?	¿Toma alcohol? *(**toh**-mah ahl-koh-**ohl**)*
Do you drink coffee?	¿Toma café? *(**toh**-mah kah-**feh**)*
Do you take vitamins?	¿Toma vitaminas? *(**toh**-mah bee-tah-**mee**-nahs)*
Did you take...	¿Tomó...? *(toh-**moh**)*
Did you take something?	¿Tomó algo? *(toh-**moh ahl**-goh)*
Did you take medicine?	¿Tomó medicina? *(toh-**moh** meh-dee-**see**-nah)*
Did you take the wrong medicine?	¿Tomó la medicina incorrecta? *(toh-**moh** lah meh-dee-**see**-naheen-koh-**rrehk**-tah)*

Did you take too much medicine? | ¿Tomó demasiada medicina?
*(toh-**moh** deh-mah-see-**ah**-dah meh-dee-**see**-nah)*

Did you take illegal drugs? | ¿Tomó drogas ilegales?
*(toh-**moh** **droh**-gahs ee-lee-**gah**-les)*

Did you drink alcohol? | ¿Tomó alcohol?
*(toh-**moh** ahl-koh-**ohl**)*

Did you vomit? | ¿Vomitó?
*(boh-mee-**toh**)*

Do you smoke? | ¿Fuma?
*(**foo**-mah)*

Can you...? | ¿Puede...?
*(poo-**eh**-deh)*

Can you hear me? | ¿Puede oirme?
*(poo-**eh**-deh oh-**eer**-meh)*

Can you talk? | ¿Puede hablar?
*(poo-**eh**-deh ah-**blahr**)*

Can you move? | ¿Puede moverse?
*(poo-**eh**-deh moh-**behr**-seh)*

Can you walk? | ¿Puede caminar?
*(poo-**eh**-deh kah-mee-**nahr**)*

Can you breathe? | ¿Puede respirar?
*(poo-**eh**-deh reh-speer-**ahr**)*

Can you squeeze? | ¿Puede apretar?
*(poo-**eh**-deh ah-preh-**tahr**)*

Can you squeeze my hand? | ¿Puede apretar mi mano?
*(poo-**eh**-deh ah-preh-**tahr** mee **mah**-noh)*

Are you... | ¿Está...?
*(eh-**stah**)*

Are you congested? | ¿Está congestionado(a)?
*(eh-**stah** kohn-heh-stee-oh-**nah**-doh(ah))*

Do you smoke?	¿Fuma? (**foo**-mah)
Can you...?	¿Puede...? (poo-**eh**-deh)
Can you hear me?	¿Puede oirme? (poo-**eh**-deh oh-**eer**-meh)
Can you talk?	¿Puede hablar? (poo-**eh**-deh ah-**blahr**)
Can you move?	¿Puede moverse? (poo-**eh**-deh moh-**behr**-seh)
Can you walk?	¿Puede caminar? (poo-**eh**-deh kah-mee-**nahr**)
Can you breathe?	¿Puede respirar? (poo-**eh**-deh reh-speer-**ahr**)
Can you squeeze?	¿Puede apretar? (poo-**eh**-deh ah-preh-**tahr**)
Can you squeeze my hand?	¿Puede apretar mi mano? (poo-**eh**-deh ah-preh-**tahr** mee **mah**-noh)
Are you...	¿Está...? (eh-**stah**)
Are you congested?	¿Está congestionado? (eh-**stah** kohn-heh-stee-oh-**nah**-doh(ah))
Are you bleeding?	¿Está sangrando? (eh-**stah** sahn-**grahn**-doh)
Are you tired?	¿Está cansado(a)? (eh-**stah** kahn-**sah**-doh(ah))
Are you dizzy?	¿Está mareado(a)? (eh-**stah** mah-reh-**ah**-doh(ah))
Are you pregnant?	¿Está embarazada? (eh-**stah** ehm-bah-rah-**sah**-dah)

Are you having a reaction?	¿Está teniendo una reacción? *(eh-**stah** teh-nee-**ehn**-doh oo-nah reh-ahk-see-**ohn**)*
Are weak or tired?	¿Está débil o cansado(a)? *(eh-**stah** **deh**-beel oh kahn-**sah**-doh(dah))*
Have you been...?	¿Ha estado...? *(ah eh-**stah**-doh)*
Have you been sneezing?	¿Ha estado estornudando? *(ah eh-**stah**-doh eh-stohr-noo-**dahn**-doh)*
Have you been coughing?	¿Ha estado tosiendo? *(ah eh-**stah**-doh toh-see-**ehn**-doh)*
Have you been sleeping?	¿Ha estado durmiendo? *(ah eh-**stah**-doh dohr-mee-**ehn**-doh)*
Have you been eating?	¿Ha estado comiendo? *(ah eh-**stah**-doh koh-mee-**ehn**-doh)*
Have you been drinking?	¿Ha estado tomando? *(ah eh-**stah**-doh toh-**mahn**-doh)*
Did you hit...?	¿Se dió...? *(seh dee-**oh**)*
Did you hit your head?	¿Se dió en la cabeza? *(seh dee-**oh** ehn lah kah-**beh**-sah)*
Did you hit yourself with something?	¿Se dió con algo? *(seh dee-**oh** kohn **ahl**-goh)*
Do you know?	¿Sabe? *(**sah**-beh)*
Do you know where you are?	¿Sabe dónde está? *(**sah**-beh **dohn**-deh eh-**stah**)*
Do you know your name?	¿Sabe su nombre? *(**sah**-beh soo **nohm**-breh)*
Do you know your address?	¿Sabe su dirreción? *(**sah**-beh soo dee-rehk-see-**ohn**)*

Lesson 4

Ejercicios: Questions for the Patient (Preguntas para el Paciente)

A. Patient # 1. Find out...

1. ...where it hurts. →

_____

2. ... what this person ate. →

_____

3. ... if he / she wants something to eat. →

_____

4. ... if he / she needs to go to the bathroom. →

_____

5. ... if this person has difficulty urinating. →

_____

6. ... if this person took medicine. →

_____

7. ... if this person vomited. →

_____

8. ... if this person feels week or tired. →

_____

9. ... if this person hit him/herself with something. →

_____

10. ... if this person knows his/her name. →

_____

Patient # 2. Find out...

1. ... if it hurts. →

_____

2. ... if it hurts a lot or a little. →

_____

3. ... if somebody hurt this person. →

_____

4. ... if this person was ever unconscious. →

_____

5. ... what were this person's symptoms. →

_____

6. ... how it happened. →

_____

7. ... if this person fell. →

_____

8. ... if this person has chills. →

_____

9. ... if this person has back pain. →

_____

10. ... if this person is taking any medicines. →

_____

Patient # 3. Find out...

1. ... if this person knows his her address. →

_____

2. ... if this person knows his / her name. →

_____

3. ... if this person knows where he / she is. →

_____

4. ... if this person can squeeze your hand. →

_____

5. ... if this person can hear you. →

_____

6. ... if this person can move. →

_____

7. ... if this person took something. →

_____

8. ... if this person took illegal drugs. →

_____

9. ... if this person has pain. →

_____

10. ... how this person feels. →

_____

Patient # 4. Find out...

1. ... if it hurts when you press. →

_____

2. ... where the weapon is. →

_____

3. ... when it happened. →

_____

4. ... how many hours (he/she has been like this). →

_____

5. ... how much this person weighs. →

_____

6. ... how long ago (something happened). →

_____

7. ... in what part. →

_____

8. ... if this person wants to go to the hospital. →

_____

9. ... if this person has numbness. →

_____

10. ... if this person is cold. →

_____

Patient # 5. Find out...

1. ... if this person took the wrong medicine. →

_____

2. ... if this person took too much medicine. →

_____

3. ... if this person drank alcohol. →

_____

4. ... if this person is having a reaction. →

_____

5. ... if this person has been sneezing. →

_____

6. ... if this person has been eating. →

_____

7. ... if this person has been drinking. →

_____

8. ... if this person has been sleeping. →

_____

9. ... if this person hit his / her head. →

_____

10. ... if this person is dizzy. →

_____

Patient # 6. Find out...

1. ... if the person is pregnant. →

_____

2. ... if the person is tired. →

_____

3. ... if the person is bleeding. →

_____

4. ... if the person can breathe. →

_____

5. ... if the person can walk. →

_____

6. ... if the person takes any pills. →

_____

7. ... if the person has any difficulty swallowing. →

_____

8. ... if the person has any difficulty defecating. →

_____

9. ... if the person has contractions. →

_____

10. ... if the person has alleries to any medicines. →

_____

Patient # 7. Find out...

1. ... if the person has a problem. →

_____

2. ... if it was an accident. →

_____

3. ... if the person has nausea. →

_____

4. ... if the person has chest pain. →

_____

5. ... if the person has a headache. →

_____

6. ... if the person needs to go to the hospital. →

_____

7. ... if the person wants something to drink. →

_____

8. ... if the person wants something. →

_____

9. ... where it hurts. →

_____

10. ... if the person wants something for pain. →

_____

Patient # 8. Ask the patient...

1. ... where he /she is. →

_____

2. ... what is happening to him / her. →

_____

3. ... how much time. →

_____

4. ... how often. →

_____

5. ... when something started.

_____

6. ... what he / she was doing. →

_____

7. ... how many pills. →

_____

8. ... how many days. →

_____

9. ... how many weeks. →

_____

10. ... what he /she ate / drank. →

_____

Patient # 9. Ask the patient...

1. ... if he / she needs an appointment. →

_____

2. ... if he / she has any allegies. →

_____

3. ... if he / she has any allergies to penicillin. →

_____

4. ... if he has any testicular pain. →

_____

5. ... if he / she has any stomach pain. →

_____

6. ... if he / she has any difficulty breathing. →

_____

7. ... if he /she takes any pills. →

_____

8. ... if he / she drinks any alcohol. →

_____

9. ... if he / she drinks any coffee. →

_____

10. ... if he / she takes any vitamins. →

_____

Patient # 10. Ask the patient...

1. ... if he / she can talk. →

_____

2. ... if he / she is hungry. →

_____

3. ... if he / she is thirsty. →

_____

4. ... if he / she is hot. →

_____

5. ... if he / she takes any medicines. →

_____

6. ... if he / she took any illegal drugs. →

_____

7. ... if he / she smokes. →

_____

8. ... if he / she is congested. →

_____

9. ... if he / she has been coughing. →

_____

10. ... if he /she has any difficulty. →

_____

B. Remember how to say?...

1....Show me. →

_____

2. ... a lot or a little? →

_____

3....How many? →

_____

4. ...What? →

_____

5. ... your symptoms. →

_____

6.... Do you need? →

_____

7.... Do you take? →

_____

8.... Can you? →

_____

9. ...How often? →

_____

10. ...Do you want? →

_____

C. Match the two columns.

1. Do you know your address?	a. ¿Quiere algo de comer?
2. Did you hit yourself with something?	b. ¿Tiene contracciones?
3. Have you been drinking?	c. ¿Cómo se siente?
4. Are you having a reaction?	d. ¿Tiene frío?
5. Can you squeeze my hand?	e. ¿Toma drogas ilegales?
6. Did you take too much medicine?	f. ¿Está teniendo una reacción?
7. Are you pregnant?	g. ¿Tomó demasiada medicina?
8. Can you hear me?	h. ¿Sabe su dirección?
9. Do you take illegal drugs?	i. Enséñeme dónde le duele.
10. Are you cold?	j. ¿Cuándo empezó?
11. Do you have difficulty urinating?	k. ¿Qué comió?
12. Do you have back pain?	l. ¿Necesita una cita?
13. Do you have chills?	m. ¿Tiene dolor de pecho?
14. Do you need an appointment?	n. ¿Tiene dolor de espalda?
15. Do you have chest pain?	o. ¿Está embarazada?
16. Was it an accident?	p. ¿Tiene escalofríos?
17. How do you feel?	q. ¿Se dio con algo?
18. Do you have contractions?	r. ¿Ha estado tomando?
19. Do you want something to eat?	s. ¿Le duele cuando presiono?
20. What is happening to you?	t. ¿Qué le pasa?
21. What did you eat?	u. ¿Fue un accidente?
22. When did it start?	v. ¿Tiene dificultad para orinar?
23. Does it hurt when I press?	w. ¿Puede oirme?
24. Show me where it hurts.	x. ¿Puede apretar mi mano?
25. Where is the weapon?	y. ¿Dónde está el arma?

D. Do it again! (Match the columns.)

1. ¿Sabe su nombre?	a. Where does it hurt?
2. ¿Ha estado durmiendo?	b. Did someone hurt you?
3. ¿Se dio en la cabeza?	c. When did it happen?
4. ¿Ha estado estornudando?	d. How much do you weigh?
5. ¿Está sangrando?	e. Were you unconscious?
6. ¿Tomó drogas ilegales?	f. How many weeks?
7. ¿Puede respirar?	g. Do you want something to drink?
8. ¿Toma alcohol?	h. Do you want something for the pain?
9. ¿Tiene dificultad para defecar?	i. Do you want to go to the hospital?
10. ¿Tiene dolor en los testículos?	j. Do you need to go to the bathroom?
11. ¿Tiene dolor de cabeza?	k. Do you have a problem?
12. ¿Tiene alergias?	l. Do you have nausea?
13. ¿Necesita ir al baño?	m. Do you have allergies?
14. ¿Tiene un problema?	n. Do you have a headache?
15. ¿Quiere ir al hospital?	o. Do you have testicular pain?
16. ¿Estaba inconsciente?	p. Do you have difficulty defecating?
17. ¿Cuánto pesa?	q. Do you drink alcohol?
18. ¿Quiere algo para el dolor?	r. Did you take illegal drugs?
19. ¿Lo / la lastimó alguien?	s. Can you breathe?
20. ¿Dónde le duele?	t. Are you bleeding?
21. ¿Cuándo ocurrió?	u. Have you been sneezing?
22. ¿Cuántas semanas?	v. Do you know your name?
23. ¿Quiere algo de tomar?	w. Did you hit your head?
24. ¿Tiene náusea?	x. Have you been sleeping?
25. ¿Toma medicinas?	y. Do you take medicines?

E. Put the words in order to make meaningful sentences.

1. respirar? / ¿Tiene / para / dificultad → _____

2. de / dolor / ¿Tiene / estómago? → _____

3. comiendo? / estado / ¿Ha → _____

4. poco? / o / ¿Le / mucho / duele → _____

5. duele / dónde / Enséñeme / le → _____

6. presiono? / ¿Le / cuando / duele → _____

7. síntomas? / son / ¿Cuáles / sus → _____

8. adormecimiento? / ¿Tiene → _____

9. ¿Necesita / hospital? / ir / al → _____

10. medicinas? / ¿Tiene / a / algunas / alergias→

_____

F. Now, translate the sentences you just made.

1. _____

2. _____

3. _____

4. _____

5. _____

6. _____

7. _____

8. _____

9. _____

10. _____

LESSON 5

Treatment (El Tratamiento)

I'm going to...	Voy a... (**boh**-ee ah)
listen to your lungs	escuchar los pulmones (eh-skoo-**chahr** lohs pool-**moh**-nehs)
I'm going to listen to your lungs.	Voy a escuchar los pulmones. (**boh**-ee ah eh-skoo-**chahr** lohs pool-**moh**-nehs)
take your pulse	tomarle el pulso (toh-**mahr**-leh ehl **pool**-soh)
I'm going to take your pulse.	Voy a tomarle el pulso. (**boh**-ee ah toh-**mahr**-leh ehl **pool**-soh)
take your blood pressure	tomarle la presión sanguínea (toh-**mahr**-leh lah preh-see-**ohn** sahn-**gee**-neh-ah)
I'm going to take your blood pressure.	Voy a tomarle la presión sanguínea. (**boh**-ee ah toh-**mahr**-leh lah preh-see-**ohn** sahn-**gee**-neh-ah)
take your temperature	tomarle la temperatura (toh-**mahr**-leh lah tehm-peh-rah-**too**-rah)
I'm going to take your temperature.	Voy a tomarle la temperatura. (boh-**ee** ah toh-**mahr**-leh lah tehm-peh-rah-**too**-rah)
give you oxygen	darle oxígeno (**dahr**-leh ohk-**see**-heh-noh)
I'm going to give you oxygen.	Voy a darle oxígeno. (**boh**-ee ah **dahr**-leh ohk-**see**-heh-noh)
give you a prescription	darle una receta (**dahr**-leh **oon**-ah reh-**see**-tah)
put on a bandage	ponerle un vendaje (poh-**nehr**-leh oon behn-**dah**-heh)
I'm going to put on a bandage.	Voy a ponerle un vendaje. (**boh**-ee ah poh-**nehr**-leh oon behn-**dah**-heh)
apply pressure	aplicarle presión (ah-plee-**kahr**-leh preh-see-**ohn**)

I'm going to apply pressure.	Voy a aplicarle presión. (*boh*-ee ah ah-plee-*kahr*-leh preh-see-*ohn*)
wash it	lavarlo(a) (lah-*bahr*-loh(lah))
I'm going to wash it.	Voy a lavarlo(a). (*boh*-ee ah lah-*bahr*-loh(lah))
give you an injection	ponerle una inyección (poh-*nehr*-leh **oo**-nah een-yehk-see-*ohn*)
I'm going to give you an injection.	Voy a ponerle una inyección. (*boh*-ee ah poh-*nehr*-leh **oo**-nah een-yehk-see-*ohn*)
put you on a stretcher	ponerle en la camilla (poh-*nehr*-leh ehn lah kah-*mee*-yah)
I'm going to put you on a stretcher.	Voy a ponerle en la camilla. (*boh*-ee ah poh-*nehr*-leh ehn lah kah-*mee*-yah)
take you to the hospital	llevarle al hospital (yeh-*bahr*-leh ahl oh-spee-*tahl*)
I'm going to take you to the hospital.	Voy a llevarle al hospital. (*boh*-ee ah yeh-*bahr*-leh ahl oh-spee-*tahl*)
refer you to another doctor	referirle a otro(a) doctor(a) (reh-feh-*reer*-leh ah oh-troh(ah) dohk-*tohr*(ah))
I am going to refer you to another doctor.	Voy a referirle a otro(a) doctor(a). (*boh*-ee ah reh-feh-*reer*-leh ah **oh**-troh dohk-*tohr*)
You need...	Necesita... (neh-seh-*see*-tah)
You need stiches.	Necesita puntos. (neh-seh-*see*-tah **poon**-tohs)
You need a cast.	Necesita un yeso (neh-seh-*see*-tah oon **yeh**-soh)

You need an emergency operation.	Necesita una operación de emergencia.
	*(neh-seh-**see**-tah oo-nah oh-peh-rah-see-**ohn** deh eh-mehr-**hehn**-see-ah)*
You need to go to the hospital.	Necesita ir al hospital.
	*(neh-seh-**see**-tah eer ahl oh-speh-**tahl**)*
talk on your cell phone	hablar por su teléfono celular
	*(ah-**blahr** pohr teh-**leh**-foh-noh sehl-oo-**lahr**)*
You need to wait for the ambulance.	Necesita esperar por la ambulancia.
	*(neh-seh-**see**-tah eh-speh-**rahr** pohr lah ahm-boo-**lahn**-see-ah)*
You need to see the doctor.	Necesita ver al doctor.
	*(neh-seh-**see**-tah behr ahl dohk-**tohr**)*
You need to take this medicine.	Necesita tomar esta medicina.
	*(neh-seh-**see**-tah toh-**mahr** eh-stah meh-dee-**see**-nah)*
You need to rest.	Necesita descansar.
	*(neh-seh-**see**-tah deh-skahn-**sahr**)*
You need to have these tests done.	Necesita hacerse estos exámenes.
	*(neh-seh-**see**-tah ah-**sehr**-seh **eh**-stohs ehk-**sah**-meh-nehs)*
You need to come back.	Necesita regresar.
	*(neh-seh-**see**-tah reh-greh-**sahr**)*

Lesson 5

Ejercicios: Treatment (El Tratamiento)

A. Finish the sentences with an appropriate expression from the box.

a darle oxigeno	tomar esta medicina	a tomarle la temperatura
hacerse estos exámenes	puntos	llevarle al hospital
tomarle el pulso	un yeso	escuchar sus pulmones
aplicarle presión	regresar	tomarle la presión
a darle una receta	ver al doctor	al hospital
	sanguínea	

1. Voy a _____ → I am going to listen to your lungs.

2. Voy _____ → I am going to give you oxygen.

3. Necesita _____ → You need stitches.

4. Necesita _____ → You need to take this medicine.

5. Necesita _____ → You need to have these tests done.

6. Voy a _____ → I am going to take your pulse.

7. Voy _____ → I am going to take your temperature.

8. Voy a _____ → I am going to take you to the hospital.

9. Necesita _____ → You need a cast.

10. Voy a _____ → I am going to apply pressure.

11. Voy _____ → I am going to give you a prescription.

12. Necesita ir _____ → You need to go to the hospital.

13. Necesita _____ → You need to come back.

14. Voy a _____ → I am going to take your blood pressure.

15. Necesita _____ → You need to see the doctor.

B. Tell your patient...

1. ... that you are going to put on a bandage. →

_____

2. ... that you are going to wash it. →

_____

3. ... that you are going to give him / her an injection. →

_____

4. ... that you are going to put him / her on a stretcher. →

_____

5. ... that you are going to refer him / her to another doctor. →

_____

6. ... that he / she needs an emergency operation. →

_____

7. ... that he / she needs to wait for the ambulance. →

_____

8. ... that he / she needs to rest. →

_____

9. ... that you are going to apply pressure. →

_____

10. ...that you are going to give him / her oxygen. →

_____

C. *Voy a...* or *Necesita*? Choose the correct begining for every sentence.

Voy a... → **I am going to...**
Necesita... → **You need...**

1. _____ escuchar los pulmones.

2. _____ tomarle el pulso.

3. _____ una operación de emergencia.

4. _____ ponerle en la camilla.

5. _____ aplicarle presión.

6. _____ un yeso.

7. _____ referirle a otro doctor.

8. _____ ver al doctor.

9. _____ descansar.

10. _____ ponerle una inyección.

D. Now, translate the sentences you just built.

1. _____

2. _____

3. _____

4. _____

5. _____

6. _____

7. _____

8. _____

9. _____

10. _____

E. Unscramble the words to make meaningful sentences.

1. presión / a / Voy / tomarle / la / sanguínea.

_____

2. temperatura / Voy / tomarle / la / a.

_____

3. receta / a / Voy / una / darle.

_____

4. Voy / ponerle / a / vendaje / un.

_____

5. inyección / una / ponerle / Voy / a.

_____

6. hospital / llevarle / a / al / Voy.

_____

7. estos / hacerse/ Necesita / exámenes.

_____

8. medicina / esta / tomar / Necesita.

_____

9. Necesita / ambulancia / esperar / por / la.

_____

10. regresar / Necesita.

_____

F. Now, translate the sentences you just built.

1. _____
2. _____
3. _____
4. _____
5. _____
6. _____
7. _____
8. _____
9. _____
10. _____

TREATMENT

G. Choose (from the box) the correct translation for these expressions and write it in the space provided.

Necesita puntos.   Voy a tomarle la presión sanguínea.   Necesita regresar.

Voy a darle una receta.   Voy a ponerle una inyección.   Voy a darle oxígeno.

Voy a lavarlo(a).   Necesita un yeso.   Voy a tomarle la temperatura.

Voy a ponerle un vendaje.   Voy a ponerle en la camilla.

Necesita ir al hospital.   Necesita hacerse estos exámenes.

Necesita una operación de emergencia.   Necesita esperar por la ambulancia.

Necesita tomar esta medicina.   Voy a tomarle el pulso.

Voy a llevarle al hospital. Voy a escuchar los pulmones. Voy a aplicarle presión.

---

1. I'm going to take your blood pressure. →

_____

2. You need a cast. →

_____

3. You need to take this medicine. →

_____

4. I'm going to listen to your lungs. →

_____

5. I'm going to put you on a stretcher. →

_____

6. You need to come back. →

_____

7. I'm going to take your temperature. →

_____

8. You need stiches. →

_____

9. You need to go to the hospital. →

_____

10. I'm going to give you oxygen. →

_____

11. I'm going to wash it. →

_____

12. You need to wait for the ambulance. →

_____

13. I'm going to take your pulse. →

_____

14. I'm going to put on a bandage. →

_____

15. You need to have these tests done. →

_____

16. I'm going to apply pressure. →

_____

17. I'm going to give you an injection. →

_____

18. You need an emergency operation. →

_____

19. I'm going to take you to the hospital. →

_____

20. I'm going to give you a prescription. →

_____

H. Study the pronunciation section in your vocabulary. Say out loud these words in Spanish, transcribe them into Spanish and also write what they mean in English.

1. ***boh**-ee ah* →

_____ /

_____

2. ***boh**-ee ah **dahr**-leh **oon**-ah reh-**see**-tah* →

_____ /

_____

3. *neh-seh-**see**-tah deh-skahn-**sahr*** →

_____ /

_____

4. ***boh**-ee ah reh-feh-**reer**-leh ah **oh**-troh dohk-**tohr*** →

_____ /

_____

5. ***boh**-ee ah toh-**mahr**-leh lah preh-see-**ohn** sahn-**gee**-neh-ah* →

_____ /

_____

6. *neh-seh-**see**-tah **oo**-nah oh-peh-rah-see-**ohn** deh eh-mehr-**hehn**-see-ah* →

_____ /

_____

7. *neh-seh-**see**-tah reh-greh-**sahr*** →

_____ /

_____

8. ***boh**-ee ah **dahr**-leh ohk-**see**-heh-noh* →

_____ /

_____

9. *neh-seh-**see**-tah **poon**-tohs* →

_____ /

_____

10. *neh-seh-**see**-tah eh-speh-**rahr** pohr lah ahm-boo-**lahn**-see-ah* →

_____ /

_____

11. ***boh**-ee ah eh-skoo-**chahr** lohs pool-**moh**-nehs* →

_____ /

_____

12. *neh-seh-**see**-tah toh-**mahr** eh-stah meh-dee-**see**-nah* →

_____ /

_____

13. *neh-seh-**see**-tah oon **yeh**-soh* →

_____ /

_____

14. ***boh**-ee ah poh-**nehr**-leh **oo**-nah een-yehk-see-**ohn*** →

_____ /

_____

15. *neh-seh-**see**-tah ah-**sehr**-seh eh-stohs ehk-**sah**-meh-nehs* →

_____ /

_____

16. ***boh**-ee ah toh-**mahr**-leh ehl **pool**-soh* →

_____ /

_____

17. *boh-**ee** ah toh-**mahr**-leh lah tehm-peh-rah-**too**-rah* →

_____ /

_____

18. ***boh**-ee ah poh-**nehr**-leh ehn lah kah-**mee**-yah* →

_____ /

_____

19. *neh-seh-**see**-tah behr ahl dohk-**tohr*** →

_____ /

_____

20. *neh-seh-**see**-tah eer ahl oh-speh-**tahl*** →

_____ /

_____

LESSON 6

An Accident (Un Accidente)

What happened?	¿Qué pasó? (*keh* pah-*soh*)
He/she stopped breathing.	Paró de respirar. (pah-*roh* deh reh-spee-*rahr*)
He/she was hit by a car.	Le atropelló un auto. (leh ah-troh-peh-*yoh* oon ah-*oo*-toh)
He/she was shot.	Le dispararon. (leh dee-spah-*rah*-rohn)
He/she had a heart attack.	Tuvo un ataque al corazón. (*too*-boh oon ah-*tah*-keh ahl koh-rah-*sohn*)
He/she is poisoned.	Está envenenado (a). (eh-*stah* ehn-beh-neh-*nah*-doh(ah))
He/she was electrocuted.	Se electrocutó. (seh eh-lehk-troh-koo-*toh*)
He/she was burned.	Se quemó. (seh keh-*moh*)
He/she drowned.	Se ahogó. (seh ah-oh-*goh*)
He/she fell.	Se cayó. (seh kah-*yoh*)
He/she fainted.	Se desmayó. (seh deh-smah-*yoh*)
He/she died.	Se murió. (seh moo-ree-*oh*)
He/she was bitten.	Fue mordido. (foo-*eh* mohr-*dee*-doh)
He/she was bitten by a dog.	Fue mordido por un perro. (foo-*eh* mohr-*dee*-doh pohr oon *peh*-rroh)

He/she was bitten by a snake.	Fue mordido por una serpiente. *(foo-eh mohr-dee-doh pohr oo-nah sehr-pee-ehn-teh)*
He/she was stabbed.	Fue apuñalado(a). *(foo-eh ah-poo-nyah-lah-doh(ah))*
He/she was raped.	Fue violado(a). *(foo-eh bee-oh-lah-dah(oh))*
He/she is having an allergy attack.	Tiene un ataque de alergias. *(tee-eh-neh oon ah-tah-keh deh ah-lehr-hee-ahs)*
He/she is having an asthma attack.	Tiene un ataque de asma. *(tee-eh-neh oon ah-tah-keh deh ah-smah*
He/she overdosed.	Tiene una sobre dosis. *(tee-eh-neh oo-nah soh-breh doh-sees)*
He/she took illegal drugs.	Tomó drogas ilegales. *(toh-moh droh-gahs ee-lee-gah-lehs)*
Which kind of illegal drug?	¿Cuál tipo de droga ilegal? *(koo-ahl tee-poh deh droh-gah ee-lee-gahl)*
heroin	heroina *(eh-roh-ee-nah)*
crack	crack *(krahk)*
marijuana	marihuana *(mah-ree-oo-ah-nah)*
cocaine	cocaína *(koh-kah-ee-nah)*
He/she is...	Está... *(eh-stah)*
conscious	consciente *(kohn-see-ehn-teh)*
unconscious	inconsciente *(een-kohn-see-ehn-teh)*

in a coma	en estado de coma *(ehn eh-**stah**-doh deh **koh**-mah)*
having convulsions	convulsionando *(kohn-bool-see-oh-**nahn**-doh)*
bleeding	sangrando *(sahn-**grahn**-doh)*

Lesson 6

Ejercicios: An Accident (Un Accidente)

A. ¿Qué pasó? (What happened?)

1. He / she was stabbed. → _____

2. He / she is bleeding. → _____

3. He /she overdosed. → _____

4. He / she died. → _____

5. He /she had a heart attack. → _____

6. He she drowned. → _____

7. He / she is in a coma. →_____

8. He / she is having an asthma attack. → _____

9. He /s he is having convulsions. → _____

10. He / she was raped. →_____

B. What is the correct ending of these sentences? Circle the correct answer.

1. Le atropelló...	a. electrocutó	b. envenenado	c. un auto
2. Fue mordido...	a. respirar	b. por un perro	c. por un auto
3. Tiene un ...	a. inconsciente	b. ataque de alergias	c. estado de coma
4. ¿Cuál tipo de...	a. droga ilegal	b. asma	c. una serpiente
5. Paró de ...	a. envenenado	b. respirar	c.inconsciente
6. Tuvo un ...	a. auto	b. serpiente	c. ataque al corazón
7. Está...	a. cayó	b. envenenado	c. quemó
8. Fue mordido...	a. al corazón	b. por un auto	c. por una serpiente
9. Está...	a. inconsciente	b. crack	c. mordido
10. Le...	a. respirar	b. consciente	c.dispararon

C. Say what happened to these people? ("y" means "and")

1. Le atropelló un auto y está sangrando.

_____

2. Se electrocutó y se quemó.

_____

3. Tuvo un ataque al corazón y se murió.

_____

4. Fue mordido por una serpiente y se desmayó.

_____

5. Tomó drogas ilegales y está inconsciente.

_____

6. Fue mordido y está consciente.

_____

7. Se cayó y paró de respirar.

_____

8. Le dispararon y se desmayó.

_____

9. Le apuñalaron y está convulsionando.

_____

10. Tiene una sobredosis y paró de respirar.

_____

D. Unscramble the letters to make these terms for illegal drugs.

1. A / O / C / C / N / A / I →

_____

2. C / K / A / R / C →

_____

3. A / H / M / A / N / A / I / R / U →

_____

4. A / H / O / R / I / N / E →

_____

E. Study the pronunciation section in your vocabulary. Say these words out loud in Spanish, transcribe them into Spanish and also write what they mean in English.

1. *too-boh oon ah-tah-keh ahl koh-rah-sohn* →

_____ /

_____

2. *foo-eh bee-oh-lah-dah(oh)* →

_____ /

_____

3. *eh-stah een-kohn-see-ehn-teh* →

_____ /

_____

4. *tee-eh-neh oo-nah soh-breh doh-sees* →

_____ /

_____

5. *seh deh-smah-yoh* →

_____ /

_____

6. *pah-**roh** deh reh-spee-**rahr*** →

_____ /

_____

7. *foo-**eh** mohr-**dee**-doh pohr oon **peh**-rroh* →

_____ /

_____

8. *koo-**ahl** tee-poh deh **droh**-gah ee-lee-**gahl*** →

_____ /

_____

9. *foo-**eh** mohr-**dee**-doh pohr **oo**-nah sehr-pee-**ehn**-teh* →

_____ /

_____

10. *leh ah-troh-peh-**yoh** oon ah-**oo**-toh* →

_____ /

_____

11. *tee-**eh**-neh oon ah-**tah**-keh deh ah-**lehr**-hee-ahs* →

_____ /

_____

12. *seh ah-oh-**goh*** →

_____ /

_____

13. *mah-ree-oo-**ah**-nah* →

_____ /

_____

14. *eh-**stah** sahn-**grahn**-doh* →

_____ /

_____

15. *tee-**eh**-neh oon ah-**tah**-keh deh **ah**-smah* →

_____ /

_____

AN ACCIDENT

16. *eh-**stah** ehn-beh-neh-**nah**-doh(ah)* →

_____ /

_____

17. *eh-roh-**ee**-nah* →

_____ /

_____

18. *seh moo-ree-**oh*** →

_____ /

_____

19. *keh pah-**soh*** →

_____ /

_____

20. *toh-**moh droh**-gahs ee-lee-**gah**-lehs* →

_____ /

_____

70   ©KAMMS Consulting, LLC

LESSON 7

Pregnancy (El Embarazo)

She is having a baby.	Ella está dando a luz. (*eh*-yah eh-***stah dahn***-doh ah loos)
Are you pregnant?	¿Está embarazada? (*eh-**stah** ehm-bah-rah-**sah**-dah*)
your last period	su último periodo (*soo **ool**-tee-moh peh-ree-**oh**-doh*)
When was your last period?	¿Cuándo fue su último periodo? (*koo-**ahn**-doh foo-**eh** soo **ool**-tee-moh peh-ree-**oh**-doh*)
children	hijos (***ee**-hohs*)
How many children do you have?	¿Cuántos hijos tiene? (*koo-**ahn**-tohs **ee**-hohs tee-**eh**-neh*)
pregnancies	embarazos (*ehm-bah-**rah**-sohs*)
Were your pregnancies normal?	¿Fueron sus embarazos normales? (*foo-**eh**-rohn soos ehm-bah-**rah**-sohs nohr-**mah**-lehs*)
miscarriage	aborto natural (*ah-**bohr**-toh nah-too-**rahl***)
Did you have a miscarriage?	¿Ha tenido un aborto natural? (*ah teh-**nee**-doh oon ah-**bohr**-toh nah-too-**rahl***)
Do you have...?	¿Tiene...? (*tee-**eh**-neh*)
Do you have a headache?	¿Tiene dolor de cabeza? (*tee-**ehn**-eh doh-**lohr** deh kah-**beh**-sah*)
Do you have swelling?	¿Tiene hinchazón? (*tee-**ehn**-eh een-chah-**sohn***)
Do you have cramps?	¿Tiene calambres? (*tee-**ehn**-eh kah-**lahm**-brehs*)

Do you have back pain?	¿Tiene dolor de espalda? *(tee-**ehn**-eh doh-**lohr** deh eh-**spahl**-dah)*
Are you vomiting?	¿Está vómitando? *(eh-**stah boh**-mee-tahn-doh)*
Are you bleeding?	¿Está sangrando? *(eh-**stah** sahn-**grahn**-doh)*
your water	la bolsa de agua *(lah **bohl**-sah deh **ah**-goo-ah)*
Did your water break?	¿Se le rompió la bolsa de agua? *(seh leh rohm-pee-**oh** lah **bohl**-sah deh **ah**-goo-ah)*
contractions	contracciones *(kohn-trahk-see-**oh**-nehs)*
Are you having contractions?	¿Tiene contracciones? *(tee-**eh**-neh kohn-trahk-see-**oh**-nehs)*
When did your contractions begin?	¿Cuándo comenzaron las contracciones? *(koo-**ahn**-doh koh-mehn-**sah**-rohn lahs kohn-trahk-see-**oh**-nehs)*
dilating	dilatando *(dee-lah-**tahn**-doh)*
You're dilating.	Está dilatando. *(eh-**stah** dee-lah-**tahn**-doh)*
You're fully dialated.	Está totalmente dilatada. *(eh-**stah** toh-tahl-**mehn**-teh dee-lah-**tah**-dah)*
labor	el parto *(ehl **pahr**-toh)*
We need to induce labor.	Tenemos que inducirle el parto. *(teh-**neh**-mohs keh een-doo-**seer**-leh ehl **pahr**-toh)*
Do you want an epidural?	¿Quiere la epidural? *(kee-**eh**-reh **oo**-nah eh-pee-doo-**rahl**)*
Push!	¡Empuje! *(ehm-**poo**-heh)*

Breathe!	¡Respire! *(reh-**spee**-reh)*
There are complications.	Hay complicaciones. *(**ah**-ee kohm-plee-kah-see-**oh**-nehs)*
The baby is doing fine.	El(la) bebé está bien. *(ehl (lah) beh-**beh** eh-**stah** **bee**-ehn)*

Lesson 7

Ejercicios: Pregnancy (El Embarazo)

A. Ask the patient the correct questions in Spanish.

1. You want to know if all her pregnancies were normal. →

_____

2. You want to know if she ever had a miscarriage. →

_____

3. You want to know if she has any swelling. →

_____

4. You want to know if she has any cramps. →

_____

5. You want to know if she has a headache. →

_____

6. You want to know if she has any back pain. →

_____

7. You want to know if she is bleeding. →

_____

8. You want to know if she is vomiting. →

_____

9. You want to know if she is having contractions. →

_____

10. Ask when the contractions began. →

_____

B. These sentences have some missing words. Fill them in choosing words from the box below.

rompió	contracciones	totalmente
inducirle	periodo	dando a luz
hijos	embarazada	epidural

1. Está _____ dilatada. → You are fully dialated.

2. Tenemos que _____ el parto. → We need to induce labor.

3. ¿Se le _____la bolsa de agua? → Did your water break?

4. ¿Cuándo comenzaron las _____? →

When did your contractions begin?

5. ¿Cuántos _____tiene? → How many children do you have?

6. ¿Cuándo fue su último _____? → When was your last period?

7. ¿Está _____? → Are you pregant?

8. Ella está _____. → She is having a baby.

9. ¿Quiere la _____? → Do you want an epidural?

C. Now, translate the sentences you just built.

1. _____

2. _____

3. _____

4. _____

5. _____

6. _____

7. _____

8. _____

9. _____

10. _____

D. Quick thinking! Your patient is ready to deliver! Tell her these things.

1. You are dilating. →

_____

2. Do you want an epidural? →

_____

3. Push! →

_____

4. Breathe! →

_____

5. There are complications. →

_____

6. The baby is fine. →

_____

E. Finish these sentences choosing an appropriate ending from the options given.

1. ¿Tiene ...   a. dilatada?   b. bolsa de agua?   c.dolor de cabeza?

2. ¿Cuándo ...   a. el parto?   b. fue su último periodo?   c.hijos tiene?

3. El (la) bebé está ...   a. embarazada.   b. dilatada.   c.bien.

4. ¿Tiene ...   a. contracciones?   b. sangrando?   c.vomitando?

5. Tenemos que ...   a. la epidural   b. la bolsa de agua   c. inducirle el parto.

6. ¿Cuántos ...   a. dolor de cabeza? b. hijos tiene?   c. calambres?

7. ¿Fueron sus embarazos... a. hijos?   b. último periodo?   c. normales?

8. Hay ...   a. sangrando   b. complicaciones   c. dolor de espalda.

9. ¿Se le rompió...   a. la bolsa de agua? b. la cabeza?   c. la epidural?

10. ¿Ha tenido...   a. vomitando?   b. el parto?   c. un aborto natural?

F. Now, translate the sentences you just built.

1. _____
2. _____
3. _____
4. _____
5. _____
6. _____
7. _____
8. _____
9. _____
10. _____

G. Back to basics. How do you say these words?

1. LABOR →

2. CRAMPS →

3. PREGNANT →

4. COMPLICATIONS →

5. FINE →

6. MISCARRIAGE →

7. CONTRACTIONS →

8. PERIOD →

9. CHILDREN →

10. BLEEDING →

11. SWELLING →

12. DILATING →

13. EPIDURAL →

14. PUSH! →

15. HEADACHE →

16. YOUR WATER →

17. PREGNANCIES →

18. BACK PAIN →

19. BREATHE! →

20. VOMITING →

21. NORMAL PREGNANCIES →

22. FULLY DIALATED →

23. BABY →

24. LAST PERIOD →

25. DO YOU HAVE...? →

H. Study the pronunciation section in your vocabulary. Transcribe these words/expressions into Spanish and also write what they mean in English.

1. *ehl (lah) beh-**beh** eh-**stah bee**-ehn.* →

_____ /

_____

2. *tee-**eh**-neh kohn-trahk-see-**oh**-nehs* →

_____ /

_____

3. *seh leh rohm-pee-**oh** lah **bohl**-sah deh **ah**-goo-ah* →

_____ /

_____

4. ***eh**-yah eh-**stah dahn**-doh ah loos* →

_____ /

_____

5. ***ee**-hohs* →

_____ /

_____

6. *eh-**stah** dee-lah-**tahn**-doh* →

_____ /

_____

7. *ehl **pahr**-toh* →

_____ /

_____

8. *ehm-**poo**-heh* →

_____ /

_____

9. *ehm-bah-**rah**-sohs* →

_____ /

_____

10. *ah-**bohr**-toh nah-too-**rahl*** →

_____ /

_____

11. *reh-**spee**-reh* →

_____ /

_____

12. *tee-**ehn**-eh doh-**lohr** deh kah-**beh**-sah* →

_____ /

_____

13. *koo-**ahn**-tohs **ee**-hohs tee-**eh**-neh* →

_____ /

_____

14. *soo **ool**-tee-moh peh-ree-**oh**-doh* →

_____ /

_____

15. *eh-**stah** sahn-**grahn**-doh* →

_____ /

_____

LESSON 8

Parts of the Body (Partes del Cuerpo)

head	cabeza (kah-**beh**-sah)
hair	pelo (**peh**-loh)
face	cara (**kah**-rah)
lip	labio (**lah**-bee-oh)
eye lid	párpado (**pahr**-pah-doh)
eye	ojo (**oh**-hoh)
jaw	mandíbula (mahn-**dee**-boo-lah)
nose	nariz (nah-**rees**)
mouth	boca (**boh**-kah)
teeth	dientes (dee-**ehn**-tehs)
tongue	lengua (**lehn**-goo-ah
throat	garganta (gahr-**gahn**-tah)
neck	cuello (koo-**eh**-yoh)
ear	oreja (oh-**reh**-hah)

inner ear	oído *(oh-**ee**-doh)*
shoulder	hombro *(**ohm**-broh)*
arm	brazo *(**brah**-soh)*
elbow	codo *(**koh**-doh)*
finger	dedo *(**deh**-doh)*
hand	mano *(**mah**-noh)*
chest	pecho *(**peh**-choh)*
back	espalda *(eh-**spahl**-dah)*
knee	rodilla *(roh-**dee**-yah)*
leg	pierna *(pee-**ehr**-nah)*
ankle	tobillo *(toh-**bee**-yoh)*
foot	pie *(**pee**-eh)*
toe	dedo del pie *(**deh**-doh dehl **pee**-eh)*
rib	costilla *(koh-**stee**-yah)*
bellybutton	ombligo *(ohm-**blee**-goh)*

waist	cintura *(seen-**too**-rah)*
hip	cadera *(kah-**deh**-rah)*
artery	arteria *(ahr-**teh**-ree-ah)*
vein	vena *(**beh**-nah)*
cartilage	cartílago *(kahr-**tee**-lah-goh)*
tendon	tendón *(tehn-**dohn**)*
ligament	ligamento *(lee-gah-**mehn**-toh)*
kidney	riñón *(ree-**nyohn**)*
heart	corazón *(koh-rah-**sohn**)*
lung	pulmón *(pool-**mohn**)*
liver	hígado *(**ee**-gah-doh)*
pancreas	páncreas *(**pahn**-kreh-ahs)*
stomach	estómago *(eh-**stoh**-mah-goh)*
uterus	útero *(**oo**-teh-roh)*
bladder	vejiga *(beh-**hee**-gah)*

ovary	ovario *(oh-**bah**-ree-oh)*
testes	testículo *(teh-**stee**-koo-loh)*
intestine	intestino *(een-teh-**stee**-noh)*
blood	sangre *(**sahn**-greh)*
bone	hueso *(oo-**eh**-soh)*
skin	piel *(pee-**ehl**)*
muscle	músculo *(**moo**-skoo-loh)*
nerve	nervio *(**nehr**-bee-oh)*
spinal cord	espina dorsal *(eh-**spee**-nah dohr-**sahl**)*
brain	cerebro *(seh-**reh**-broh)*
spleen	bazo *(**bah**-soh)*
appendix	apéndix *(ah-**pehn**-deex)*
gall bladder	vesícula biliar *(beh-**see**-koo-lah bee-lee-**ahr**)*
kidney	riñón *(ree-**nyohn**)*
heart	corazón *(koh-rah-**sohn**)*

Lesson 8

Ejercicios: Parts of the Body (Partes del Cuerpo)

A. Guess!

1. Your hands have 10 of these. → D _ _ _ _

2. You use it to smell. → N _ _ _ _

3. It covers all your body. → P _ _ _

4. It filters your blood. → R _ _ _ _

5. It pumps blood everywhere in your body. → C _ _ _ _ _ _ _

6. Nervous system component. → N _ _ _ _ _

7. Digests food. → E _ _ _ _ _ _ _

8. Skeletal system component. → H _ _ _ _

9. You use it to hear. → O _ _ _ _

10. You have 2 and they have 10 toes. → P _ _

B. Match the two columns.

1. Appendix   a. Pecho
2. Intestine   b. Hombro
3. Bladder   c. Testículos
4. Artery   d. Vesícula biliar
5. Gall bladder   e. Garganta
6. Belly button   f. Apéndice
7. Chest   g. Oído
8. Eye lid   h. Intestino
9. Leg   i. Ombligo
10. Throat   j. Vejiga
11. Testes   k. Arteria
12. Spleen   l. Párpado
13. Cartilage   m. Pierna
14. Shoulder   n. Bazo
15. Inner ear   o. Cartílago
16. Spinal cord   p. Páncreas
17. Lung   q. Ovario
18. Waist   r. Espina dorsal
19. Pancreas   s. Pulmón
20. Ovary   t. Cintura

C. Identify (from the list of words given) all of the terms that make reference to parts of the face.

tobillo	ojo	costilla	ombligo	dientes
nariz	pierna	labio	mandíbula	lengua
hombro	boca	brazo	cara	hígado
ovario	brazo	tendón		

1._____   5._____

2._____   6._____

3._____   7._____

4._____   8._____

D. Unscramble the letters to make the words for these parts of the body.

1. Z / A / B / A / C / E → _____HEAD

2. S / P / E / A / L / D / A → _____ BACK

3. S / Ó / E / T / O / M / A G → _____ STOMACH

4. A / S / I / C / O / T / L / L → _____ RIB

5. Z / R / A / B / O → _____ARM

6. B / C / R / O / E / E / R → _____ BRAIN

7. I / H / G / D / A / O → _____ LIVER

8. D / A / C / E / R / A / → _____ HIP

9. G / S / E / R / N / A → _____ BLOOD

10. N / Ó / D / E / T / N → _____ TENDON

E. Fill in the vocabulary columns.

1. LIGAMENTO   _____

2. _____   MUSCLE

3. DEDO DEL PIE   _____

4. CUELLO   _____

5. _____   ANKLE

6. PELO   _____

7. _____   ELBOW

8. _____   UTERUS

9. VENA   _____

10. MANO   _____

11. _____   KNEE

F. Review this lesson's vocabulary and look for cognates. (Cognates are words that look & sound similar in Spanish & English)

1. _____   8. _____

2. _____   9. _____

3. _____   10. _____

4. _____   11. _____

5. _____   12. _____

6. _____   13. _____

7. _____   14. _____

G. Definitions. Read the definitions for the body parts and write the Spanish word for them.

1. The part of the human trunk between the bottom of the rib cage and the pelvis.

_____

2. The part of the human body between the neck and upper arm.

_____

3. A major part of the central nervous system which conducts sensory and motor nerve impulses to and from the brain.

_____

4. The fleshy, movable, muscular organ, attached to the floor of the mouth that is the principal organ of taste.

_____

5. The fluid consisting of plasma, blood cells, and platelets that is circulated by the heart through the vascular system, carrying oxygen and nutrients to and waste materials away from all body tissues.

_____

6. The navel.

_____

7. Part of the body that consists of the wrist, palm, four fingers, and thumb.

_____

8. The chambered muscular organ that pumps blood.

_____

9. Tissue that forms the external covering of humans.

_____

10. The organ of hearing.

_____

11. This connects the foot with the leg.

_____

24. Also called "womb".

_____

25. Central nervous system organ enclosed in the cranium.

_____

H. Study the pronunciation section in your vocabulary. Transcribe these words/expressions into Spanish and also write what they mean in English.

1. *beh-**see**-koo-lah bee-lee-**ahr*** →

_____ /

_____

2. *tehn-**dohn*** →

_____ /

_____

3. ***deh**-doh dehl **pee**-eh* →

_____ /

_____

4. ***ee**-gah-doh* →

_____ /

_____

5. ***nehr**-bee-oh* →

_____ /

_____

6. *kah-**beh**-sah* →

_____ /

_____

7. ***peh**-choh* →

_____ /

_____

8. beh-**hee**-gah →

_____ /

_____

9. kah-**deh**-rah →

_____ /

_____

10. dee-**ehn**-tehs →

_____ /

_____

11. roh-**dee**-yah →

_____ /

_____

12. eh-**stoh**-mah-goh →

_____ /

_____

13. oo-**eh**-soh →

_____ /

_____

14. **beh**-nah →

_____ /

_____

15. **lah**-bee-oh →

_____ /

_____

16. **oh**-hoh →

_____ /

_____

17. koo-**eh**-yoh→

_____ /

_____

18. **bah**-soh →

_____ /

_____

19. teh-**stee**-koo-loh →

_____ /

_____

20. ah-**pehn**-deex → _____ /

_____

21. **brah**-soh →

_____ /

_____

22. gahr-**gahn**-tah →

_____ /

_____

23. oh-**ee**-doh →

_____ /

_____

24. **pahn**-kreh-ahs →

_____ /

_____

25. een-teh-**stee**-noh →

_____ /

_____

ANSWER KEY

Lesson 1: Commands (Mandatos)

A. Tell a patient...
1. Cierre los ojos.
2. Respire profundo.
3. Enrolle la manga.
4. Relájese.
5. Trate de dormir.
6. No llore.
7. Descanse
8. No se preocupe.
9. Siéntese.
10. Dígame qué pasó.

B. Identify, from the list of words given, all of the terms that make reference to <u>body parts</u>.
1. Acuéstese de espalda.
2. Saque la lengua.
3. Doble el brazo.
4. Abra los ojos.
5. Póngalo debajo de la lengua.
6. Cierre los ojos.
7. Doble la pierna.
8. Cierre la boca.

C. Translate the suggested sentences by making combinations with expressions from columns A and B.
1. Póngalo debajo.
2. Respire despacio.
3. Siéntese aquí.
4. Venga aquí.
5. Camine normalmente.
6. Acuéstese aquí.
7. Espere afuera.
8. Mire para arriba.
9. Respire profundo.
10. Voltéese despacio.
11. Vaya afuera.
12. Mire para abajo.
13. Venga despacio.
14. Camine asi.
15. Siéntese afuera.
16. Mire para atrás.

D. Choose the most appropriate option to finish the sentences.
1. Espere un momento.
2. Quédese en la cama.
3. Siga las instrucciones.
4. Tome la medicina.
5. Quítese su camisa.

E. Now, translate the sentences you just built. The first letter of the verb is already written.
1. Wait a moment.
2. Stay in bed.
3. Follow the instructions.
4. Take the medicine.
5. Take off your shirt.

F. Fill in the missing vowels to make these basic commands.
1. LEVÁNTESE
2. PARE
3. DÍGAME
4. DÉME
5. ESCRIBA
6. MUÉVASE
7. DOBLE
8. EMPUJE
9. SILENCIO
10. QUÉDESE
11. CIERRE
12. ABRA
13. SAQUE
14. TRÁGUESE
15. TOSA
16. TOQUE
17. SEÑALE
18. ENSEÑE
19. TRATE
20. DESPIÉRTESE

G. Match the two columns.
1. f	8. m	15. g	22. p
2. d	9. e	16. h	23. t
3. o	10. s	17. c	24. a
4. v	11. n	18. u	25. j
5. i	12. r	19. l	
6. k	13. b	20. w	
7. y	14. q	21. x	

H. Study the pronunciation section in your vocabulary. Say the words in Spanish, transcribe them into Spanish and write what they mean.

1. voltéese / turn over
2. no toque / don't touch
3. escriba / write
4. abra / open
5. cuidado / be careful
6. deme / give me
7. tráguese / swallow
8. enseñe / show
9. no se levante / don't stand up
10. muévase / move
11. enrolle la manga / roll up your sleeve
12. espéreme / wait for me
13. respire así / breathe like this
14. señale / point to
15. pare eso / stop that
16. quedése quieto / stay still
17. despiértese / wake up
18. siéntese aquí / sit here
19. no empuje / don't push
20. tosa / cough
21. siga / follow
22. diga "ah" / say "ah"
23. doble el brazo / bend your arm
24. relájese / relax

Lesson 2: Meeting the Patient (*La Reunión con el Paciente*)
A. Fill in the blank with the correct word to complete the sentences.

1. b – bien
2. c – Hable
3. d – Necesito
4. c – ayudar
5. a – preguntas
6. d – Quién
7. b – Hablo
8. b - entiendo
9. c - Soy
10. d - enfermo
11. b – Por qué
12. c - Puedo
13. a - necesario
14. a - lastimado
15. d - Cómo

B. Unscramble the words to make meaningful sentences.

1. ¿Quién necesita ayuda?
2. Soy el (la) doctor.
3. No es importante.
4. Necesito examinarlo (la).
5. Todo está bien.
6. ¿Por qué está aqui?
7. ¿Quién está lastimado (a)?
8. Hablo un poco de español.
9. ¿Cómo se llama?
10. Soy el (la) ayudante.

C. Now, translate the sentences you just built.

1. Who needs help?
2. I am the doctor.
3. It is not important.
4. I need to examine you.
5. Everything is fine.
6. Why are you here?
7. Who is hurt?
8. I speak a little Spanish.
9. What is your name?
10. I am the assistant.

D. *I can help!* Exchange the first words with a car accident victim.

1. Me llamo...
2. Hablo un poco de español.
3. Soy el (la) paramédico.
4. Vamos a ayudar.
5. ¿Está lastimado(a)?
6. Necesito examinarlo(a).
7. Es necesario.
8. Tengo preguntas.
9. Hable despacio.
10. No entiendo.
11. Está bien.

E. Choose, from the box, the English version of the words provided.

1. Help.
2. I can help.
3. I am the nurse.
4. I am the assitant.
5. I don't understand.
6. It is not important.
7. Why?
8. Speak slowly.
9. I have questions.
10. Everything is fine.

F. Ask the right questions! Choose the most appropriate question for every situation.

1. b.   6. a.
2. c.   7. c.
3. a.   8. c.
4. a.   9. a.
5. b.   10. b.

G. Study the pronunciation section in your vocabulary. Say the words in Spanish, transcribe them into Spanish and write what they mean in English.

1. ¿Está bien? / Are you OK? OR Está bien / You are doing fine.
2. Soy el (la) doctor(a) / I am the doctor.
3. No es importante. / It is not important.
4. ¿Cómo se llama? / What is your name?
5. Me llamo... / My name is...
6. Tengo preguntas / I have questions.
7. ¿Necesita ayuda? / Do you need help?
8. Hablo un poco de español / I speak a little Spanish.
9. Vamos a ayudar / We are going to help.
10. Necesito examinarlo(a) / I need to examine you.
11. No entiendo. / I don't understand.
12. ¿Está lastimado(a)? / Are you hurt?
13. Soy el (la) ayudante. / I am the assistant.
14. Hable despacio. / Speak slowly.
15. Es necesario. / It is necessary.
16. ¿Habla inglés? / Do you speak English?
17. ¿Por qué está aquí? / Why are you here?
18. Todo está bien. / Everything is fine.
19. ¿Quién necesita ayuda? / Who needs help?
20. Soy el (la) enfermero(a). / I am the nurse.

Lesson 3: What the Patient Would Say (*Qué Diría el Paciente*).
A. What are they telling you?

1. c   6. b
2. c   7. c
3. b   8. b
4. c   9. c
5. b   10. b

B. You are the patient now. Say in Spanish...

1. ¡Ayuda!   6. Necesito...
2. Tengo dolor fuerte.   7. Quiero...
3. Me duele mucho aquí.   8. ¿Usted sabe?
4. Me caí.   9. ¿Qué hace?
5. No puedo respirar.   10. No sé.

C. Predict the statements you will get from a patient in these situations.
Answers may vary slightly. Some appropriate examples are...

1. Me duele / Me duele mucho / Me duele   6. No puedo.
aquí.   7. Está sangrando.
2. Me pica aquí.   8. Me quema / me quema aquí.
3. Está enferma.   9. Está lastimado(a).
4. No puedo dormir.   10. ¡Ayúdale!
5. ¿Me voy a morir?

94   ©KAMMS Consulting, LLC

D. Choose, from the box, the correct translation for these expressions and write it in the space provided.

1. He/she fell.
2. I have an allergy.
3. I can't sleep.
4. It hurts when I breathe.
5. I have chest pain.
6. I can't move.
7. Do you know?
8. I am bleeding.
9. Help!
10. It burns here.

11. I am sick.
12. Am I going to die?
13. I am afraid.
14. I have pain.
15. I can't breathe.
16. What are you doing?
17. It itches here.
18. I can't eat.
19. I have severe pain.
20. I am hurt.

E. Study the pronunciation section in your vocabulary. Say out loud these words in Spanish, transcribe them into Spanish and also write what they mean in English.

1. ¡Ayudame! / Help me!
2. Sangre / blood
3. No sé. / I don't know.
4. No puedo. / I can't.
5. Me duele mucho. / It hurts a lot.
6. Está enfermo(a). / He/she is sick.
7. Me quema. / It burns.
8. ¡Ayúdale! / Help him/her!
9. Necesito... / I need...
10. ¿Se va a morir? / Is he/she going to die?

12. Me duele. / It hurts.
13. Me pica. / It itches.
14. Está sangrando. / He/she is bleeding.
15. Me duele aquí. / It hurts here.
16. Está lastimado(a). / He/she is hurt.
17. Quiero... / I want...
18. dolor / pain
19. Se cayó. / He/she fell.
20. ¿Qué hace? / What are you doing?

Lesson 4: Questions for the Patient. *(Preguntas para el Paciente)*
A. Patient # 1. Find out...

1. ¿Dónde le duele?
2. ¿Qué comió?
3. ¿Quiere algo de comer?
4. ¿Necesita ir al baño?
5. ¿Tiene dificultad para orinar?

6. ¿Tomó medicina?
7. ¿Vomitó?
8. ¿Está débil o cansado(a)?
9. ¿Se dio con algo?
10. ¿Sabe su nombre?

Patient # 2. Find out...

1. ¿Le duele?
2. ¿Le duele mucho o poco?
3. ¿Lo / la lastimó alguien?
4. ¿Estaba inconsciente?
5. ¿Cuáles son sus síntomas?

6. ¿Cómo ocurrió?
7. ¿Se cayó?
8. ¿Tiene escalofrios?
9. ¿Tiene dolor de la espalda?
10. ¿Toma medicinas?

Patient # 3. Find out...

1. ¿Sabe su dirección?
2. ¿Sabe su nombre?
3. ¿Sabe dónde está?
4. ¿Puede apretar mi mano?
5. ¿Puede oirme?

6. ¿Puede moverse?
7. ¿Tomó algo?
8. ¿Tomó drogas ilegales?
9. ¿Tiene dolor?
10. ¿Cómo se siente?

Patient # 4. Find out...

1. ¿Le duele cuando presiono?
2. ¿Dónde está el arma?
3. ¿Cuándo ocurrio?
4. ¿Cuántas horas?
5. ¿Cuánto pesa?

6. ¿Por cuánto tiempo?
7. ¿En qué parte?
8. ¿Quiere ir al hospital?
9. ¿Tiene adormecimiento?
10. ¿Tiene frío?

Patient # 5. Find out...
1. ¿Tomó la medicina incorrecta?
2. ¿Tomó demasiada medicina?
3. ¿Tomó alcohol?
4. ¿Está teniendo una reacción?
5. ¿Ha estado estornudando?

6. ¿Ha estado comiendo?
7. ¿Ha estado tomando?
8. ¿Ha estado durmiendo?
9. ¿Se dio en la cabeza?
10. ¿Está mareado(a)?

Patient # 6. Find out...
1. ¿Está embarazada?
2. ¿Está cansado(a)?
3. ¿Está sangrando?
4. ¿Puede respirar?
5. ¿Puede caminar?

6. ¿Toma pastillas?
7. ¿Tiene dificultad para tragar?
8. ¿Tiene dificultad para defecar?
9. ¿Tiene contracciones?
10. ¿Tiene alergias a algunas medicinas?

Patient # 7. Find out...
1. ¿Tiene un problema?
2. ¿Fue un accidente?
3. ¿Tiene náusea?
4. ¿Tiene dolor en el pecho?
5. ¿Tiene dolor de cabeza?

6. ¿Necesita ir al hospital?
7. ¿Quiere algo de tomar?
8. ¿Quiere algo?
9. ¿Dónde le duele?
10. ¿Quiere algo para el dolor?

Patient # 8. Ask the patient...
1. ¿Dónde está?
2. ¿Qué le pasa?
3. ¿Cuánto tiempo?
4. ¿Con qué frecuencia?
5. ¿Cuándo empezó?

6. ¿Qué estaba haciendo?
7. ¿Cuántas pastillas?
8. ¿Cuántos dias?
9. ¿Cuántas semanas?
10. ¿Qué tomó?

Patient # 9. Ask the patient...
1. ¿Necesita una cita?
2. ¿Tiene alergias?
3. ¿Tiene alergia a la penicilina?
4. ¿Tiene dolor en los testículos?
5. ¿Tiene dolor de estómago?

6. ¿Tiene dificultad para respirar?
7. ¿Toma pastillas?
8. ¿Toma alcohol?
9. ¿Toma café?
10. ¿Toma vitaminas?

Patient # 10. Ask the patient...
1. ¿Puede hablar?
2. ¿Tiene hambre?
3. ¿Tiene sed?
4. ¿Tiene calor?
5. ¿Toma medicinas?

6. ¿Tomó drogas ilegales?
7. ¿Fuma?
8. ¿Está congestionado(a)?
9. ¿Ha estado tosiendo?
10. ¿Tiene dificultad?

B. Remember how to say...
1. Enséñeme.
2. ¿... mucho o poco?
3. ¿Cuántos?
4. ¿Qué?
5. ... sus síntomas.

6. ¿Necesita...?
7. ¿Toma...?
8. ¿Puede...?
9. ¿Con qué frecuencia?
10. ¿Quiere...?

C. Match the two columns.

1. h
2. q
3. r
4. f
5. x
6. g
7. o
8. w
9. e
10. d
11. v
12. n
13. p

14. l
15. m
16. u
17. c
18. b
19. a
20. t
21. k
22. j
23. s
24. i
25. y

D. Do it again!

1. v
2. x
3. w
4. u
5. t
6. r
7. s
8. q
9. p
10. o
11. n
12. m

13. j
14. k
15. i
16. e
17. d
18. h
19. b
20. a
21. c
22. f
23. g
24. l
25. y

E. Put the words in order to make meaningful sentences.

1. ¿Tiene dificultad para respirar?
2. ¿Tiene dolor de estómago?
3. ¿Ha estado comiendo?
4. ¿Le duele mucho o poco?
5. Enséñeme dónde le duele.
6. ¿Le duele cuando presiono?
7. ¿Cuáles son sus síntomas?
8. ¿Tiene adormecimiento?
9. ¿Necesita ir al hospital?
10. ¿Tiene alergias a algunas medicinas?

F. Now, translate the sentences you just made.

1. Do you have difficulty breathing?
2. Do you have a stomachache?
3. Have you been eating?
4. Does it hurt a lot or a little?
5. Show me where it hurts.
6. Does it hurt when I press?
7. What are your symptoms?
8. Do you have numbness?
9. Do you need to go to the hospital?
10. Do you have allergies to any medicines?

Lesson 5. Treatment (*El Tratamiento*)
A. Finish the sentences with an appropriate expression from the box.

1. ... escuchar sus pulmones.
2. ... a darle oxigeno.
3. ... puntos.
4. ... tomar esta medicina.
5. ... hacerse estos exámenes.
6. ... tomarle el pulso.
7. ... a tomarle la temperatura.
8. ... llevarle al hospital.
9. ... un yeso.
10. ... aplicarle presión.
11. ... a darle una receta.
12. ... al hospital.
13. ... regresar.
14. ... tomarle la presion sanguínea.
15. ... ver al doctor.

B. Tell your patient...

1. Voy a ponerle un vendaje.
2. Voy a lavarlo(la).
3. Voy a ponerle una inyección.
4. Voy a ponerle en una camilla.
5. Voy a referirle a otro(a) doctor(a).

6. Necesita una operación emergencia.
7. Necesita esperar por la ambulancia.
8. Necesita descansar.
9. Voy a aplicarle presión.
10. Voy a darle oxigeno.

C. *Voy a...* or *Necesita*? Choose the correct begining for every sentence.

1. Voy a...
2. Voy a...
3. Necesita...
4. Voy a...
5. Voy a...

6. Necesita...
7. Voy a...
8. Necesita...
9. Necesita...
10. Voy a...

D. Now, translate the sentences you just built.

1. I am going to listen to your lungs.
2. I am going to take your pulse.
3. You need an emergency operation.
4. I am going to put you on a stretcher.
5. I am going to apply pressure.

7. I am going to refer you to another doctor.
8. You need to see the doctor.
9. You need to rest.
10. I am going to give you an injection

E. Unscramble the words to make meaningful sentences.

1. Voy a tomarle la presion sanguínea.
2. Voy a tomarle la temperatura.
3. Voy a darle una receta.
4. Voy a ponerle un vendaje.
5. Voy a ponerle una inyección.

7. Necesita hacerse estos exámenes.
8. Necesita tomar esta medicina.
9. Necesita esperar por la ambulancia.
10. Necesita regresar.

F. Now, translate the sentences you just built.

1. I am going to take your blood pressure.
2. I am going to take your temperature.
3. I am going to give you a prescription.
4. I am going to put on a bandage.
5. I am going to give you an injecction.

6. I am going to take you to the hospital.
7. You need to have these tests done.
8. You need to take this medicine.
9. You need to wait for the ambulance.
10. You need to come back.

G. Choose (from the box) the correct translation for these expressions.

1. Voy a tomarle la presión sanguínea.
2. Necesita un yeso.
3. Necesita tomar esta medicina.
4. Voy a escuchar los pulmones.
5. Voy a ponerle en la camilla.
6. Necesita regresar.
7. Voy a tomarle la temperatura.
8. Necesita puntos.
9. Necesita ir al hospital.
10. Voy a darle oxígeno.

11. Voy a lavarlo(a).
12. Necesita esperar por la ambulancia.
13. Voy a tomarle el pulso.
14. Voy a ponerle un vendaje.
15. Necesita hacerse estos exámenes.
16. Voy a aplicarle presión.
17. Voy a ponerle una inyección.
18. Necesita una operación de emergencia.
19. Voy a llevarle al hospital.
20. Voy a darle una receta.

H. Study the pronunciation section in your vocabulary. Say out loud these words in Spanish, transcribe them into Spanish and also write what they mean in English.

1. Voy a... / I'm going to...
2. Voy a darle una receta. / I'm going to give you a prescription.
3. Necesita descansar. / You need to rest.
4. Voy a referirle a otro(a) doctor(a). / I am going to refer you to another doctor.
5. Voy a tomarle la presión sanguínea. / I'm going to take your blood pressure.
6. Necesita una operación de emergencia. / You need an emergency operation.
7. Necesita regresar. / You need to come back.
8. Voy a darle oxígeno. / I'm going to give you oxygen.

9. Necesita puntos. / You need stiches.
10. Necesita esperar por la ambulancia. / You need to wait for the ambulance.
11. Voy a escuchar los pulmones. / I'm going to listen to your lungs.
12. Necesita tomar esta medicina. / You need to take this medicine.
13. Necesita un yeso. / You need a cast.
14. Voy a ponerle una inyección. / I'm going to give you an injection.
15. Necesita hacerse estos exámenes. / You need to have these tests done.
16. Voy a tomarle el pulso. / I'm going to take your pulse.
17. Voy a tomarle la temperatura. / I'm going to take your temperature.
18. Voy a ponerle en la camilla. / I'm going to put you on a stretcher.
19. Necesita ver al doctor. / You need to see the doctor.
20. Necesita ir al hospital. / You need to go to the hospital.

Lesson 6: An Accident (Un Accidente)
A. ¿Qué pasó? (What happened?)

1. Fue apuñalado(a).
2. Está sangrando.
3. Tiene una sobredosis.
4. Se murió.
5. Tuvo un ataque al corazón.
6. Se ahogó.
7. Está en estado de coma.
8. Tiene un ataque de asma.
9. Está convulsionando.
10. Fue violado(a).

B. What is the correct ending of these sentences?

1. c
2. b
3. b
4. a
5. b
6. c
7. b
8. c
9. a
10. c

C. Find out what happened to these pepople.

1. He / she was hit by a car and is bleeding.
2. He /she was electrocuted and was burned.
3. He / she had a heart attack and died.
4. He / she was bitten by a snake and fainted.
5. He / she took ilegal drugs and is unconscious.
6. He / she was bitten and is conscious.
7. He / she fell and stopped breathing.
8. He / she was shot and fainted.
9. He / she was stabbed and is convulsing.
10. He / she overdosed and stopped breathing.

D. Unscramble the letters to make these terms for illegal drugs.

1. Cocaína.
2. Crack.
3. Marihuana.
4. Heroína.

E. Study the pronunciation section in your vocabulary. Say out loud these words in Spanish, transcribe them into written Spanish and also write what they mean in English.

1. Tuvo un ataque al corazón. / He/she had a heart attack.
2. Fue violado(a). / He/she was raped.
3. Está inconsciente. / He/she is unconscious.
4. Tiene una sobre dosis. / He/she overdosed.
5. Se desmayó. / He/she fainted.
6. Paró de respirar. / He/she stopped breathing.
7. Fue mordido por un perro. / He/she was bitten by a dog.
8. ¿Cuál tipo de droga ilegal?/ Which kind of illegal drug?
9. Fue mordido por una serpiente. / He/she was bitten by a snake.
10. Le atropelló un auto. / He/she was hit by a car.
11. Tiene un ataque de alergias. / He/she is having an allergy attack.
12. Se ahogó. / He/she drowned.
13. marihuana / marijuana
14. Está sangrando. / He/she is bleeding.
15. Tiene un ataque de asma. / He/she is having an asthma attack.

16. Está envenenado (a). / He/she is poisoned.
17. heroína / heroin
18. Se murió. / He/she died.
19. ¿Qué pasó? / What happened?
20. Tomó drogas ilegales. / He/she took illegal drugs.

LESSON 7: Pregnancy (*El Embarazo*)
A. Ask the patient the correct questions.
1. ¿Fueron sus embarazos normales?
2. ¿Ha tenido un aborto natural?
3. ¿Tiene hinchazón?
4. ¿Tiene calambres?
5. ¿Tiene dolor de cabeza?
6. ¿Tiene dolor de espalda?
7. ¿Está sangrando?
8. ¿Está vomitando?
9. ¿Tiene contracciones?
10. ¿Cuándo comenzaron las contracciones?

B. These sentences have some missing words. Fill them in choosing words from the box.
1. ...totalmente...
2. ...inducirle...
3. ...rompió...
4. ...contracciones?
5. ...hijos...
6. ...periodo?
7. ...embarazada?
8. ...dando a luz.
9. ...epidural?

C. Now, translate the sentences you just built.
1. You are fully dialated.
2. We need to induce labor
3. Did your water break?
4. When did your contractions begin?
5. How many children do you have?
6. When was your last period?
7. Are you pregant?
8. She is having a baby.
9. Do you want an epidural?

D. Quick thinking! Your patient is ready to deliver! Tell her these things.
1. Está dilatando.
2. ¿Quiere la epidural?
3. ¡Empuje!
4. ¡Respire!
5. Hay complicaciones.
6. El bebe está bien.

E. Finish these sentences choosing an appropriate ending from the options given.
1. c
2. b
3. c
4. a
5. c
6. b
7. c
8. b
9. a
10. c

F. Now, translate the sentences you just built.
1. Do you have a headache?
2. When was your last period?
3. The baby is doing fine.
4. Are you having contractions?
5. We need to induce labor.
6. How many children do you have?
7. Were your pregnancies normal?
8. There are complications.
9. Did your water break?
10. Did you have a miscarriage?

G. Back to basics. How do you say these words?

1. Parto.
2. Calambres.
3. Embarazada.
4. Complicaciones.
5. Bien.
6. Aborto natural.
7. Contracciones.
8. Período.
9. Hijos.
10. Sangrando.
11. Hinchazón.
12. Dilatando.
13. Epidural.
14. ¡Empuje!
15. Dolor de cabeza.
16. La bolsa de agua.
17. Embarazos.
18. Dolor de espalda.
19. ¡Respire!
20. Vomitando.
21. Embarazos normales.
22. Totalmente dilatada.
23. Bebe.
24. Último período.
25. ¿Tiene...?

H. Study the pronunciation section in your vocabulary. Transcribe these words/expressions into Spanish and also write what they mean in English.

1. El (la) bebé está bien. / The baby is doing fine.
2. ¿Tiene contracciones? / Are you having contractions?
3. ¿Se le rompió la bolsa de agua? / Did your water break?
4. Ella está dando a luz. / She is having a baby.
5. Hijos. / Children.
6. Está dilatando. / You are dilating.
7. El parto. / Labor.
8. ¡Empuje! / Push!
9. Embarazos. / Pregancies.
10. Aborto natural. / Miscarriage.
11. ¡Respire! / Breathe!
12. ¿Tiene dolor de cabeza? / Do you have a headache?
13. ¿Cuántos hijos tiene? / How many children do you have?
14. Su último período. / Your last period.
15. ¿Está sangrando? / Are you bleeding?

Lesson 8: Parts of the Body (*Partes del Cuerpo*)
A. Guess!

1. DEDOS.
2. NARIZ.
3. PELO
4. RIÑÓN.
5. CORAZÓN.
6. NERVIO.
7. ESTÓMAGO.
8. HUESO.
9. OREJA.
10. PIE.

B. Match the two columns.

1. f
2. h
3. j
4. k
5. d
6. i
7. a
8. l
9. m
10. e
11. c
12. n
13. o
14. b
15. g
16. r
17. s
18. t
19. p
20. q

C. Choose, from the box, all the words that make reference to <u>face parts</u>.
1. Nariz
2. Mandibula
3. Ojo
4. Cara
5. Boca
6. Dientes
7. Labio
8. Lengua

D. Unscramble the letters to make the words for these parts of the body.
1. CABEZA
2. ESPALDA
3. ESTÓMAGO
4. COSTILLA
5. BRAZO
6. CEREBRO
7. HÍGADO
8. CADERA
9. SANGRE
10. TENDÓN

E. Fill in the vocabulary columns
1. LIGAMENT
2. MÚSCULO
3. TOE
4. NECK
5. TOBILLO
6. HAIR
7. CODO
8. ÚTERO
9. VEIN
10. HAND
11. RODILLA

F. Review this lesson's vocabulary and look for cognates.
1. Arteria (Artery).
2. Vena (Vein).
3. Cartílago (Cartilage).
4. Tendón (Tendon).
5. Ligamento (Ligament).
6. Páncreas (Pancreas).
7. Estómago (Stomach).
8. Útero (Uterus).
9. Ovario (Ovary).
10. Testículo (Testes).
11. Intestino (Intestine).
12. Músculo (Muscle).
13. Nervio (Nerve)
14. Apéndice (Appendix).

G. Definitions. Read the definitions for the body parts and write the Spanish word for them.
1. Cintura (waist)
2. Hombro (shoulder)
3. Espina Dorsal (spinal cord)
4. Lengua (tongue)
5. Sangre (blood)
6. Ombligo (belly button)
7. Mano (hand)
8. Corazón (heart)
9. Piel (skin)
10. Oreja (ear)
11. Tobillo (ankle)
12. Párpado (eyelid)
13. Ateria (artery)
14. Ovario (ovary)
15. Costilla (rib)
16. Riñón (kidney)
17. Pierna (leg)
18. Dedo (finger)
19. Pelo (hair)
20. Codo (elbow)
21. Cara (face)
22. Pulmón (lung)
23. Nariz (nose)
24. Útero (uterus)
25. Cerebro (brain)

H. Study the pronunciation section in your vocabulary. Say out loud these words in Spanish, transcribe them into written Spanish and also write what they mean in English.
1. Vesícula biliar / gall bladder
2. Tendón / tendon
3. Dedo del pie / toe
4. Higado / liver
5. Nervio / nerve
6. Cabeza / head
7. Pecho / chest
8. Vejiga / bladder
9. Cadera / hip
10. Dientes / teeth
11. Rodilla / knee
12. Estómago / stomach
13. Hueso / bone
14. Vena / vein
15. Labio / lip
16. Ojo / eye
17. Cuello / neck
18. Bazo / spleen
19. Testículo / testes
20. Apéndix / appendix
21. Brazo / arm
22. Garganta / throat
23. Oído / inner ear
24. Páncreas / páncreas
25. Intestino / intestine

NEW VOCABULARY & PHRASES

NEW VOCABULARY & PHRASES

KAMMS® LANGUAGE PROGRAMS*
(AUDIO CDs~DVDs~WORKBOOKS)

Spanish on the Job®

Spanish for Educators

Spanish for Law Enforcement

Spanish for Health Care

Spanish for Medical Receptionists

Spanish for Real Estate

Spanish for Retail Business

Spanish for Banking

Spanish for Human Resources

Spanish for Restaurants

Spanish for Housekeeping

Spanish for Construction

Spanish for Landscaping

Conversational Spanish

Inglés en el Trabajo® (English on the Job)

Inglés para Restaurantes (Restaurants)

Inglés para Construcción (Construction)

Inglés para Jardinería (Landscaping)

Inglés para Hospitalidad (Hospitality)

Inglés para El Trabajo Doméstico (Housekeeping)

Inglés para Oficina Médica (Medical Office)

Inglés para Limpieza y Mantenimiento (Cleaning & Maintenance)

Inglés para Educadores (Educators)

Inglés para Entrevistas de Trabajo (Job Interviews)

Inglés para Vendedores y Cajeros (Salespeople & Cashiers)

Inglés para Trabajadores Industriales (Manufacturing)

Inglés para Negocios (Business)

Inglés para Conversación (Conversational)

Other Programs

How to Become a US Citizen (English Version)

Cómo Convertirse en Ciudadano de Los Estados Unidos (Spanish Version)

And many more!
Visit us on the web to see our latest programs or sign up for our newsletter to receive language learning tips, cultural information and product announcements:

www.spanishonthejob.com
www.ingleseneltrabajo.com
866-678-0800
*CDS, DVDs & Workbooks Available on our Website & Major Retail Stores

"I wish you great success!"

Stacey Kammerman